Letters to my Brother
Year One

Boogie Brown Decker

&

Winchester Wright

Copyright © 2018 Boogie & Winchester

All rights reserved.

ISBN-13: 9781718794542
ISBN-10: 1718794541

THANK YOU

This book is written due to demand from our "Spacebook" Fans. We have had an exciting first year as you will see. We would like to thank all our fans for encouraging us to venture into this project.

We also need to thank our Moms, Kim Wright and Wendy Decker. Without them, our letters would have never been recorded. They have loved us regardless of our adventures and still manage to laugh through our trials and tribulations.

Lastly, we need to thank our readers that took their valuable time to read the draft and offered us valuable input on the contents. Our readers include; Joy Russell, Delzora Clark, Jason Spaur, Sandy Vance, and Brenda Trabosh.

Preface

To help our readers better understand the letters you will be reading, maybe we need to begin with an explanation of who we are referring to as we go along. It can be very confusing with all our relatives. As you may or may not know, we have a human family, an adoptive family, and an animal family. We love all of them very much.

Let's start with our human family they are the ones that have our Mom living with them. They are also the ones that put our pictures on "Spacebook" so our adoptive families could find us. Our human family consists of Boogie AKA Eddie, that's who I am named after and our first human Dad, Crystal is the Mama in this family and Emily is our first human sister. She loved to run and play with us and took us inside to watch TV or just lay around. She loved spoiling us. They live just outside of Farmville, North Carolina in the country with lots of room to run.

Winchester's adoptive family consists of his Mom Kim, Dad Mike, Sister Autumn, and Grandmother Mommom. He also has a dog nephew Woody AKA Chewy, Pedro, the little Mexican Kid, and Chew Wawa. His cat brother is Kenny. Kenny only has 3 legs but he sure can run. Winchester's Dad spoils him by telling him he is cute and sexy. He lets him sleep in the bed with him during the day and his Mom makes him sleep in his kennel at night. Other family you may read about in our series that have their own homes are his sister Nicole and dog nephew Optimus AKA Rotten Wyler; another sister Jen with his dog nephew Bocephus and cat nephews Chewbacca AKA Chewy, Lucky, and Garfield; and his sister Sam and his dog nephew Olaf, dog nieces, Elsa, Anna, and Maggie as well as his cat niece Kitty Kitty. It really takes a lot of people to help Winchester get through life.

My adoptive family that lives in the house with me consists of; my Mom Wendy, Dad Bennie, Nephew Tyler, dog nephew Blazzer and dog niece Sophie. My Sister Amber, Brother Chris and Sister-In-Law Dawn have their own homes. My cat nephew Little Bit has nothing to do with me. My dog neice Mama Dog AKA Mean Yellow

1

Dog and nephew Charlie live with Chris and Dawn at their house. I had to stay with them when Mom and Dad went on vacation. I like my house better because my mean brother, Chris made me listen.

This is my Author Pose

About the Authors

Winchester is on the left and Boogie on the right.

  This is a story of two brothers. My name is Boogie Brown and my brother's name is Winchester. We were born to a beautiful Chesapeake lady and a handsome Labrador man. We were from a litter of six puppies (three girls and three boys).

 Our human parents were good friends with my adoptive mom and dad and said they couldn't keep all of us so they posted pictures on a social media site called "Spacebook" or something like that. People all over the world looked at us and considered adopting us. We didn't know why they were taking these pictures and sure would not have posed so cute if we had known they were going to separate us. Our human Mom told us how we were going to new homes and would be loved and taken care of like Kings.

  My adoptive Mom (Wendy) and Dad (Bennie) came by and met me, they seemed nice enough but I still didn't want to leave my brothers and sisters. I was the first to leave, I was so sad. They brought a crate to take me home in; however, Mom couldn't let me stay in it. She held me close all the way home and I slept in her lap. A few weeks later my Dad's cousins Kim and Mike came to visit. We went back to my Human Parents' home and got Winchester. I was excited and glad to see my Mom and my other family but as before-sad to leave them.

Even though we have a great home and family, we still miss our brothers and sisters. Winchester and I are the only two that have kept up with each other. He lives in Pennsylvania with my Dad's cousins Kim and Mike while I live in North Carolina. Our parents act like that is a long ways away but Winchester and I think we could meet in the middle or something to get together more often. We missed each other so much we asked our moms to help us write letters. We told them what to say and they sent it out on that "Spacebook" thing. We have been writing for over a year now. These are some of those letters, we hope you enjoy them.

| BOOGIE | WINCHESTER |

SPRING

First Letter:

Hi Winchester,
I can't wait for you to come down for your next visit. I have been digging up the yard so we can dig to some place Dad calls China. I have also been stock piling flower pots so we can do some planting. We go to this place that has a lot more water than my fish pond (called the river). I can't drink it all, but I can bite it. I enjoy sitting in Mom and Amber's lap. Not sure what the big deal is, I only weigh a little over 40 lbs. We have got this. Until I see you next month,
Your brother, Boogie.

Yo bro!
Are they starving you? I weigh 61 pounds. My Dad calls me a lard bucket. I'm not sure if that's good or bad. Can't wait to garden with you. Mom wants to know if you want a light up collar like mine and if so, what color. She said it is easier to find me in the dark with it. Love to all.
Winchester

PS Ask Amber to teach my Mom about those selfies things. She is terrible with that phone thing she carries.

Winchester,

Sure I love fancy necklaces. Blue is my favorite color but any will do. Mom can't do selfies either. We will win Amber over. I have her right where I want her. I'm sure she would love to help your Mom. I love taking selfies with her because I can get close to her and snuggle. Love,
Boogie

Summer

Hey Winchester,
This is one of my holes. I got the rake for Dad to fill it in and brought it out while he was napping. He seems to like putting the dirt back after I dig it out.
Boogie Brown

Hey Boogie,
Is that how far China is? We got this covered. While our Dads are filling in one hole we can work on the next one. By the way, your new collar came today. It's really cool. Looks just like mine. See you soon. (Don't tell anyone, but I heard Dad tell Mom to put smoked bones on the list of stuff to bring down. They are the best).
Winchester

Hey Winchester,
Are y'all walking down here or what? I have been watching for you and can't see you. Hurry up! We had lots of rain and the ground is perfect for digging to China. Hope you like NC humidity. It can really curl our hair. It is tough but we can handle it with the Boogie pool and that thing they call a river. The boat is pretty cool too. Hurry!!
Boogie Brown

Boogie,
I have been in training this weekend. There was an invasion. I had 7 kids sleeping over and their parents and more people and kids visiting yesterday. I had to keep them all in line. Between showing

them how to properly chase balls and play in the water, I don't know how they would have done it without me. Then there were the water balloons. It was a disaster. I don't think any of them survived. (The balloons not the humans.) I really had a lot of fun with them, but I am pooped. I think I am gonna rest up today. But Dad says we'll be there next weekend, whatever that means. See you soon.
Winchester.

They call us River rats and we really love the boat. It was a very tiring day.

Hey Bro Winchester,
I hope you had a safe, easy ride home. I was sad when you left but we've got this. Already making plans for next time. We had a great time together even though they didn't understand our "ruff housing". We will train them yet. Hope to hear about your ride home and getting back to Kenny. See you soon. Love,
Boogie.

Hey Boogie,
I woke up and I was home. I looked all over and you weren't here. I even tried going back to sleep on Dad with my new toy, but you still weren't here. I think I got 'em fooled. Dad's talking about our next visit. He said maybe in October. In the meantime, see if you can get further to China in our hole. We got pretty far this week. Hope to see you soon bro. We had a blast! Love,
Winchester

PS Kenny was really glad to see Mom but I was not feeling the love. I ran up to him to say Hi and he ran under the bed. Pretty normal for Kenny but he sure gave Momma hell. (Oops heck) I think he missed her.

Hey Bro Winchester,
I have found an easier way to China. I started eating my bed and Mom said she was sending me there. Maybe you can come up with something similar and your folks will buy you a ticket too. We just have to coordinate times and make sure they send us to the same place. She mumbled something about Abudabe too. Not sure where that is but one trip at a time. Keep in touch. I can't wait to travel with you. We will have a ball! We may even dig our way back home. Just a thought. With love,
Your brother Boogie Brown.

Bro! Are you crazy? My Mom would be pitching a royal fit! She was really mad when I ate her gardening gloves and Kenny's toy. I can't imagine what would happen if I ate my bed. But that kid with the spots, Wow!!! All I can say is I hope he has good directions to that Abudabe place and gets started before his Dad gets home. I know how much trouble I was in when that pillow blew up and almost killed me. Mom didn't buy the story that I was in mortal danger and was lucky to still be alive. She acted like I was gonna be lucky to live through her temper over the pillow attacking ME! Two nights in a row! And she was even angrier the 2nd night. (I still think the kid with spots will have a hard time splaining how that sofa blew up. Humans just don't believe us poor misunderstood puppies) Love, Winchester

Dear Brother Boogie Brown,
How are those plans for Abudabe coming along? Your bed looked so tasty I decided to try it today. Needless to say, Mom was not happy. I don't think mine was the same flavor. It was all white and I was really-really thirsty til Mom got home. I must have drunk half a bowl of water. She was mumbling about Damn Decker dogs, bad habits and early Christmas decorations. I think she's really lost it this time. We may have sent her over the edge. What can we do next? Love Your brother Winchester

Hey Bro Winchester!
You did a fantastic job with your bed our trip is probably getting closer. Which do you think they will choose- China or Abudabe? I am learning a lot. You need to listen to your Mom and Dad closely. If they begin talking retirement, find them a job. This stuff is hard work. They used to leave in the morning and I had all day to do what I wanted. Now Mom may leave for 10 minutes or a few hours. I never know and always have to work fast. Protecting her is tough too. I have had to ward off the mail lady, UPS man, vacuum cleaner, a big truck blowing the horn, a few birds, the cat, and that crazy thing they use to pick things up. I forgot I also have to welcome any visitor that comes by with kisses. She is a real dare devil and I am sleep deprived keeping her safe. Love until next time,
Your Bro Boogie Brown

Dear Boogie,
I got my pool. I think it was a diversion. Tonight they took me to see this really pretty vet and I got to stay over, but before they left, Dad said it was all Moms' fault. How can staying with Dr. "she has my" Hart be a bad night??? I have to talk more later on that subject. But the pool is great. I'll keep you posted on my overnight date with Dr.

Hart. I'll bet Dad was jealous.... hehehe. One upped by his son. Bet he wishes he was me. Love, Your Casanova brother... Winchester.

Hey bro Winchester,
 I thought I warned you about that vet visit. Dr. Natalie is a beautiful lady too, but man did she get to the point! I was sore for a week. You won't be able to swim for a week either. I guess that kept her perfume smell longer. Hope you have fun with your overnight stay but I'm promising they are up to something. Nothing will ever be the same again. Keep in touch.
Your Bro Boogie Brown.

Dear Brother Boogie Brown,
My date didn't turn out like I planned. She sure was pretty but I'm missing some things a guy shouldn't need to be talking about. Mom just brought me home. Dad said it was all her fault so I'll have to wait and talk with him in the morning. I'm pretty tired tonight. Love, Winchester

Hey Bro Winchester,
I warned you, my Dad sang "Gloom despair and agony on me oohhh" – You know the HEE HAW song. It will get better and you will be ready to run and play soon, just a little lighter. If something comes up like this again, I will warn you and we can make our plans.
Boogie

Hey Winchester,
Mom and Dad took off and left me with my mean brother, Chris. He is teaching me what NO..! means and I'm doing really well with that. I've only torn up a few flower pots, been in the trash a few times, and really not liking the yellow dog. She's kinda mean. Me and Charlie (the black dog) are making friends. I think he's starting to like me. I heard you had a bad date with a pretty vet. I had one of them too. I'm sorry brother. Love you brother. Hope to hear back from you soon. Love,
 Boogie Brown

(Don't worry Boogie,
I'll bring you pig ears Sunday, and we can swap stories about our
mean brother...has he chased you into a door knob (that requires
another trip to the vet for stitches...) or trained his duck to attack you
yet? Amber)

Hey Boogie,
I need to tell you something. (I'll try to whisper. .). That yellow dog
doesn't know she's a dog. And she doesn't LIKE dogs! Please be
careful. Charlie can be testy sometimes, too. I'm sure Chris and Dawn
and the kids will defend you. Just be careful. And whatever you do,
don't give away the secret. That critter does NOT like to be called a
dog! On a happier note, you didn't tell me about the treats the pretty
vet sends home with you. Earlier today, I saw 3 tails. And they were
all mine! We won't discuss the trade off but no pain with the treats
and when Mom's not home Dad lets me nap on the bed with him. I
think Mom knows. Moms seem to know everything, More later.
Watch your six. Love,
Winchester.

Dear Winchester,
I heard my brother said I haven't been bad...LOL... I got them last
night I tore my bed into a million pieces and my brother made Caleb
clean it up. I'm having a ball while Mom and Dad are on
vacation but I do miss them a little. I do remember the treats
my pretty vet sent home with me they were awesome but
when they are gone the next couple of days are RUFF. Good
luck brother hope to hear from you soon.
Boogie

Boogie I have the Northern version of a "Boogie Pond"

Love it! Enjoy it Winchester until you can come south again. Boogie

Dear Boogie,
Does your sister let you sit on her lap to cuddle? I'm not sure how long I can milk this vet visit thing but it's working pretty well with Dad and Autumn. I still think Mom is on to me. How is your visit going? Are you running things yet? I heard Caleb is a really good cook. He's definitely someone to make up to. Love,
 Winchester

Dear Boogie,

Just a quick note while Mom is busy. Can you believe it? After I have major surgery, just because I have a few accidents in the house (that she cleaned up waaayy faster than it took her to get done yelling about it), she stopped my special treats. I was hiding behind Dad who was mumbling about red headed tempers. Can you believe that? My life is in danger and he's talking about colors, which only caused Mom to yell louder, but at least it took the heat off me. Then both of us were in trouble. So tell your Dad that if you get in trouble that he should talk about redheads. I'll bet it will work for you too. Oops. Mom's coming. Talk later.   Love, Winchester

Wow Bro Winchester,

I'm not sure what a red head is but I may need one here to keep the heat off me. I spent last week with my brother and sister in law. It was ok but I wasn't the only child so I missed being the center of the universe as Mom says often. I was glad to see them come home and am not letting them out of my sight. It is hard to keep up with these guys since they returned. I think they had a good time but now they have to make up for lost time. I am exhausted, and have to go to bed with Dad so Mom can have quiet time. I think quiet time is overrated but she enjoys it. Until next time,
Your brother Boogie Brown

Boogie,

Glad they had a good time. You keep plugging away. Play the guilt thing. They left their baby. You know the drill. Work it. Good luck bro. Love your brother,
Winchester

Dear Boogie Brown,

My Mom is a cruel woman. Yesterday and then again today I was playing with my soccer balls and by accident popped them, and then chewed up the pieces. Then I brought the pieces to Mom to clean up. Tonight she says, and I quote "well I guess you don't have any balls left". THEN she starts laughing until she can hardly breathe. I don't think she was referring to the soccer balls anymore. I think she was just being cruel. What are your thoughts on this Bro? Love, Winchester

Wow Bro Winchester,
That was a low blow if I do say so. I know your Mom didn't mean to be mean, and it was kind of funny. Might as well laugh, we must not need them anyway. Life here has fallen back into the usual, protecting Mom from all these crazy things at the house. My bed has died a slow death and I get in Mom and Dad's bed every chance I get. Don't tell Dad but some mornings Mom gives up and lets me stay. That is our secret and I am sure I can break her, not sure about Dad but I'm not giving up. She says I am a stubborn old cout. I have got to get a dictionary for some of these words or maybe a cell phone. They say Google, whatever that is, knows everything. We will work on that. Until next time, sending love your way,
Love, Bro Boogie Brown.

Dear Boogie,
Bro, I did it this time. I ate Moms sneaker. I think I've mentioned her temper a time or 2? I'm thinking I won't be getting treats for a while. I thought she'd be happy that I left Dad's sneakers alone. How was I supposed to know that I wasn't supposed to eat ANY sneakers? Just because the door was shut, was that supposed to mean keep out? I just can't keep track of all these rules. I'll keep you posted on my punishment. Love your brother,
Winchester

Wow Bro Winchester!

I'm so glad to hear from you. It must be something with the moon or something. I am having the same problem with my folks. Mom threw me out today because our furniture grew (couldn't have been me) and I was knocking stuff over. She keeps saying something about hard headed and stubborn. Soo, while I was out I did a little digging again but I got the rake for Dad. He just doesn't get how much I help him. This leave it thing is confusing. I'm not sure whether I am suppose to leave it in my mouth, where I got it, or just drop it. Guess we will have to work on this. They need to work on making themselves clearer. Hopefully, we will get them trained soon. Any suggestions you can send my way is appreciated. I still check your room occasionally to see if you have sneaked back in. Hope to see you soon. LOVE,

Your Bro Boogie Brown.

Wow Bro Winchester,

I used to grab Mom's shoes and run, but they never let me keep them long enough to chew them up. They usually grabbed them and popped me on the butt with them. Now, they always put them in that room that has the machines they put their clothes in and close the door. Their shoes are safe for now. If you need a pad to crash in, just let me know. I am sure if I look at Mom and Dad real sweet and smile, they will let you stay. We can make our battle plan if we can get together. I am sure we can handle these "adults" if we use our resources and concentrate. I'm sure you have noticed my vocabulary is growing. Since Mom is home now in the daytime she spends a lot of time talking to me. I kinda like it. She lets me nap in the day while she works. I keep an eye on her in case those big trucks or vacuum cleaner decide to attack. I would love to have backup. Keep your chin up and don't let your Mom or Dad get the best of you. You and I know they must love you a bunch! They came all the way to North Carolina to get you. Until next time, Love bunches,

Your brother Boogie Brown

Good morning Bro Winchester!
 Just thought I would let you know our trip may still be on. I was scared Mom and Dad spent all their money on their trip, but I heard Mom loud and clearly saying "it's not too late to ship you to Abudabe". I'm not sure why she was so upset. I just went hunting in the yard. I brought her a duck (That is what we are 'spose to do, isn't it?). The first day, she just mumbled and Dad put it back where it was. I thought they would be happy I found it in the flower bed and it was really heavy and hard. Not really what I thought a duck would feel like. The next day, that duck was still there so I brought it out again. That's when she starting talking about our vacation again, and telling me how old those ducks were and I had better not break them. Those stupid ducks don't move or make a sound. I think that's a little odd, but if she's happy, I am too. Don't forget to pack some cool toys for our vacation, I have eaten most of mine. Hope to see you soon. Love,
Your Bro Boogie Brown.

Boogie,
Don't you remember I told you that Mom's put really strange things in the garden for decorations. I got in big trouble the night I grabbed the turtle and ran him to the back yard. He was hard and heavy, too. Dad and some of their friends were running behind me so Mom couldn't get to me. Just be glad the duck didn't split into pieces. SMH, If it did I bet you would be seeing your Mom do more than TALK about Abudabe. As for toys , Mom said last night she is gonna start splitting the seams of the toys and taking the stuffing out before I can have them because I make such a mess. Isn't that our job? To unstuff the toys?? Well, I will keep a bag packed for our vacation and a bed ready in case you need to make a quick getaway. Love,
Your brother Winchester

Good morning Bro Winchester,
 I am understanding more and more why everyone is excited about the weekends. I get to take naps with Dad and the alarm doesn't go off so early. Monday's are tough around here. Mom and I worked all day. (I think it may have to do with me getting her up at 6) She used

that stupid vacuum cleaner again, along with the dust mop that was fun to chase. I tried to save your memories you left, but she even cleaned our nose prints off the windows. I decided to help when I knew she was going to do it no matter what. While she was cleaning the outside windows, I licked the inside. Did a great job if I do say so myself. She was speechless, but not as happy as I thought. I really get confused trying to keep up. Moms are complicated. This morning I let her sleep in until 8. I am going to figure this out soon. I'll let you know if this works. Sending love your way,
Your Bro Boogie Brown

Hey Boogie,
 Moms do love to sleep in. Mom thought she was in heaven the other morning when she slept til 8.   Hey, great news here. I'm getting a new roommate. Well, not actually my roommate, but Dad says when Mommom moves in that I can sleep with her. She does not seem to be as excited as I am, but she'll come around. I will worm my way into her heart. I'll make sure she eats and drinks. We will be buds. Wish me luck. Mom giggles and Mommom looks horrified when Dad talks about the plan.   Love,
Your bro Winchester

PS How could your Mom erase me? Be sure to help her clean those windows more. Maybe next time she will see the need for memories.

FALL

Hey Bro Winchester!
 Wow, do I have lots of things to tell you. Every time I think I know the routine, Mom and Dad change it. Dad had extra time off, but they weren't home a lot. That made me sad, but my sister came and played and tucked me in bed and fed me. I love my Amber. When they were home, we snuggled a lot except today. Wow, I heard something about Labor Day and I don't think that is good. We really worked hard. Mom pulled weeds and threw them out-I ran and got them and brought them back. I was afraid she was getting rid of something she needed. You will never guess what I found in the flower bed - another duck!!! This one is as heavy as the first and now you can have your own. I'm not sure what she is feeding these guys. I know they don't get any exercise. They just stand there and look at you. I'm working on getting mine to talk. Speaking of exercise Mom got the blower out and Dad got on the lawn mower. I ran so hard trying to protect them I had to take several dips in the Boogie Pond. By 8 o'clock I was passed out on the floor, couldn't even make it to my bed. My eyes are getting heavy, have to make a last potty run for the night and then it will be lights out. Hope your holiday was more restful than mine. Until next time, Lots of love,
 Your Bro Boogie Brown.

PS Mom is posting a picture I get no privacy as long as she has the phone close.

Bro,

Did I tell you that Dad occasionally fills one of the Grans pools for me? It's not as deep as yours but it does the trick on those hot days when you work really hard training them. Did I also tell you that Mom has been forgetting my name lately? I know she's been stressed but she keeps calling me "dammit". The dog across the street said the last dog to live here was named Dammit Buster. Maybe she's confused. But he looked more like you than me so I'm not sure. I'll send more on that later. Love,

Bro Winchester

Dear Boogie Brown,

Big weekend. Thank goodness it was busy. It's kinda took the spotlight off me eating my brand new or-tho-ped-ic bed that Dad bought for me. It was real tasty and Dad was late getting home from work and I was bored and then it blew up and I was almost killed with all the flying pieces! Dad didn't say too much but Mom repeated the name of the bed very slowly, several times, while cleaning up the mess. Good thing Mommom was moving in this weekend. She didn't have time to stay mad long. And trust me, after the sneaker incident earlier this week, she would have stayed mad. Hope you had a good weekend and you got that duck to behave. Love your brother,

Winchester

Good morning Bro Winchester!

I am in terrible trouble around here. I thought this hurricane talk would help, but not this time. Yesterday, Mom went shopping with Granny, and Cousin Debbie. It was a long day at home alone and when Dad got home I was excited. I couldn't wait for Mom to get home, because, I just knew she had bought something for me. When she got home there was nothing in those bags for me. I was disappointed and decided maybe I haven't done enough work around here. Mom and Dad went to get a pizza and I checked around. The only thing I saw that needed to be done was a little weeding like Mom and I did earlier. I pulled the only weed growing under the car port and got the pot it was in, too. I spilt a little dirt, but was sure

they would be happy. Man, you think a red headed Mom is tough, you should see mine when her eyes turn red! How was I to know she bought that weed and wanted it to stay in the planter? Man, we need a rule book to refer to. I went to bed early and laid low last night. I thought it was over this morning and what did Dad do, but remind Mom of that stupid flower weed. Now I am stuck outside again. I have plans to use my charm and win her over again soon. Lesson from this, only pull weeds with Mom. I can't tell the difference. Hope your weekend is better than mine has started. Love,
Your Brother Boogie Brown

Boogie,
 Just don't bark at the vacuum cleaner. It doesn't end well. Moms get a little nuts about that weeding stuff. Mom put this silly container in a bush that has sweet water on it. The branch tasted really good. You yanked on the branch and it sprinkled sweet water on the branches. Mom got really upset when the teeny tiny little birds stopped coming after I chewed the branch. Good luck with your Mom. Let me know if you find that rule book. Love,
Winchester

Hey Bro Boogie,
 How are you? An amazing thing happened today. I was protecting Mom from the vacuum cleaner thing and I barked at it. It barked back at me! Remember I told you about my Mom's temper? Well, she ripped this thing's head off and she held it over the trash can and dumped its insides out! She dumped its brains out! She put the head back on and did it again! Then I barked at it and she continued to push it for a while and I barked at it again and she ripped its head off and dumped its insides out again! I don't think I'll ever bark at her again!! I don't know what she'll do to me. Later she had to go to the store because Dad broke my ball shooter so she bought a new ball shooter home. Hopefully Dad won't break this one, cuz she gets pretty upset when I break my toys. She brought me home a duck. It's a rope duck and it didn't take me long but I figured if Mom could do it I could do it, so I tore its head off and ripped the stuffing out of

its head. She was not nearly as impressed with me for ripping the Ducks head off and tearing the stuffing out as I was when she ripped the vacuum cleaners head off and tore the stuffing, but I'm just wondering if your Mom rips the head off of your vacuum cleaner and throws the stuffing away. Sure hope your weekends going better.
Love,
Your brother Winchester

Well Bro Winchester,
I learned a new word today - Consequences - I don't think I like this word. I wanted to play ball this morning, but Mom said not playing was a consequence of my actions yesterday. I guess I need to back up to yesterday. Have you found that rule book yet? I swear that flower pot did not have a single flower/weed in it. How was I spose to know she was growing rocks? Mom and Granny were working on important church papers so I was outside looking for something to do. I spotted the pot. It has been there all summer, and I decided to see if China was in there. Side note, I still haven't found China. It wasn't in the bottom of that pot either. Dad laughed and said something about my poop being shiny and glowing in the dark. Is that a bad thing? I can see advantages. To come back to today, Mom spent our play time picking out the rocks and getting up the dirt from the pot. She mumbled something about consequences the whole time and wouldn't let me help. When she finished getting them up, she went inside and left me out again. My consequences were not fun. Do you know anything about that word? Hope you have had better luck with it than I have. I'm really glad Mom loves me because I'm not sure what the consequences for that would have been if she didn't. Until next time,
Your Bro Boogie Brown.

PS Mom learned the meaning of consequences today too. I knew she would feel left out if I didn't include her. The consequence of leaving me outside with the pot even if it is up on the table can be bad. I can jump and so can it. It jumped right off that table and fell over. It dumped out again! Would you believe that?

Gee Boogie,

That's a tough one. No flowers, no weeds, did you bring the rake? No, you said it was the rocks..... I got nothing. I'm still looking for the book, too. I've been kinda staying under the radar this week, except for a couple "minor" misunderstandings regarding gifts left, sometimes they don't understand. I go down to visit Mommom when she's at work, so I leave a present so she knows I was there. She has not been impressed. Maybe my poop should glow in the dark. That would have advantages. I'm still trying to win her over. So far, she is not a fan of when I jump in bed when she is sleeping at night and I sneak away from the parents. It's a work in progress. I'll win her over yet. Hang in there.

Your Bro Winchester

Boogie,

Did you wish this on me? I kinda got the idea that this consequence thing wasn't good. I didn't want an example, but that mean three legged cat, that thinks Mom is his private property decided I needed a lesson, too. I just wanted to play! I finally got him cornered. He was gonna have to play with me. I barked and jumped at him and do you know what he did?? He whomped me! That is another word that is not good. He just up and smacked my nose. It really hurt. You wouldn't believe the power behind a mean spirited cat with claws. And the worst part!!! Mom took his side! She said I told you and told you, if you don't leave him alone he is gonna whomp you one of these days. I don't like being whomped. My nose hurts. We need the rule book to see about cat brothers. Maybe he can go to China. I don't know. Mom is pretty attached to him. Maybe that's why I don't like him. Mom uses another word- JEALOUS. Not sure what it means, but she calls me Mr. Green. We'll talk of that another day.

Your bro, Winchester

Hey Winchester!

Look what I found!!! Mom and dad were cleaning the building for Dawn's birthday – that is another subject, everyone seems to have one but me, and this appeared. On to my story-look at all these balls!

It's something called pool, but mom says I can't play because I don't have thumbs. Do you have thumbs? If not, do you know where to get some? Shop around up there and see if you can find some. I will pay you. Do you think they will be expensive? Got to go they turned their back for a minute and I'm going to get one of these balls.
 Boogie

That's pretty cool, Boogie.
 Lol- But what good is your pool with no water? Those are real nice balls. Can your Dad shoot them from the gun? I never heard of thumbs, but I'll get my mom to look for them at the store, or maybe Amazon. That postman guy brings those boxes with the smiles on them. I'll bet they have thumbs. I'll have Mom check. I'm not sure about the birthday thing. We'll need to look into that.   Love, Winchester

Bro Boogie,
How have you been? Have you found them thumb things yet? I ask Dad and he gave me this funny looking thing, and Mom ....well I'm not sure what was happening. She was honking like the birds that fly in packs and her eyes were leaking and she was kinda gasping. Dad said something about a Horshack. It was very scary. My sister, Autumn, said that's what happens when Mom laughs too hard. (The honking was very weird) Anyway, apparently, a thumb Drive was not what we needed to play in your pool and I wasn't allowed to chew on it. As for the birthday thing, we have one, the same one (we are twins- actually we are more than twins, but Mom didn't know how many of

us there were. I didn't know what us she was counting) and it's in December, our birthday that is. I don't know what a December is. Maybe you can check on that part.   Until next time, Love,
Your bro Winchester

Hi Bro Winchester,
 I just got my bath and Mom says I smell really good. I didn't see anything wrong with the way I smelled before. Remember when we took a bath in the sink outside. I've graduated to the tub. I sort of like it as long as they don't get my face. No thumbs yet, it doesn't sound promising here. I have been checking on the new word you threw out that your three legged cat did. I don't think I have been whomped unless you count that dog gone rose bush thing. It seems to get me every time i get near it. Not just in the face but the butt too sometimes. I hate flower/weeds. They always get me in trouble. I wish I had a toy like Kenny the cat. As for the vacuum, I haven't witnessed a massacre here, hope you were able to find it some more brains. Usually Mom makes me go outside while she vacuums. She doesn't appreciate me helping. I was on very good graces on Saturday though. Mom was in the front yard and I saw this man in the woods across the road. I warned her and used my meanest bark and growl. Mom had not seen him. Even though it turned out she knew him and said it was ok, I kept my eye on him. She kept telling me how good I did and Dad was so proud of me. I sort laid low this weekend - no really bad trouble anyway, can you believe it? I would love to hear your Mom honk. That would be funny. Well, as for the birthday thing, Mom says there were 6 of us. Then Dad said he hoped they weren't as crazy as the two he knew about. Wonder which two he keeps up with and what has happened to the two we don't know about? I know he couldn't be talking about us. Mom says Caleb, Dad, Aunt Lisa, and Uncle Tyler all have birthdays before us. I can't wait, Mom cooks their favorite meals and Granny makes banana pudding. I love some banana pudding and it smells so good (I had it at the river when Mrs. Becky made it). They sing a song and everyone comes to see us. I love birthdays! We will

work on making ours come soon. Glad we have the same one! I'm getting tired this bath thing wears me out. Guess I'll go to bed. See you soon. Love,

Your Brother Boogie Brown

Dear Bro Boogie,

 Have I got a story for you. The other night, I ate too much cat food. And cat food is not good for dogs. So I had an "accident" in my kennel. What a mess. When Mom found it she was in the process of putting me to bed. Well, she was not pleased. So she just got a trash bag. And she threw away all of my bedding! My blankets, my toys, and she started scrubbing down my kennel. Then she asked Dad did you not smell this cage? Dad was sleeping, so he didn't smell it. So he said are you going to throw that stuff out? Aren't you going to wash it? Mom just turned around and gave Dad "the look"! It was not a good look. And, she said , I think you need to go get ready for work and Dad said, you're hurting Winchester's feelings, and she really kind of was. So Mom said to take me with him while she finished up. She was not happy. I think I'm going to be restricted from eating Kenny's food. It is really good (and it makes him really mad hehehe). I now have a beach towel to sleep with and no toys. It's like being in the prisons on TV. No toys....Until next time.

 Your bro. Winchester

P. S. Dad is not real happy with me today either. I have been looking for China and there are a few holes that Dad's tractor almost got stuck in and I couldn't find the rake. I didn't find China either. Dad said Abudabe is around the corner. I think I need to lay low this weekend.

Wow Bro Winchester!

 What a mess. That must be why my Mom puts the cat food on the front porch for those orange furry animals that live in our woods. I'm not allowed in our front yard ever. I can go all over the back even in the field, but if I head to the front, this horrible ringing goes off in my ears. It's easier to stay out back. The mail lady said she appreciated

me staying in the back, but she called me mischievous. Something about things I am doing when she comes by. I've been doing a little duck hunting in the yard. Remember the two I told you about? One suffered a serious accident. It was something about a broken neck. Dad said I did it, but it was like that when he picked it up. He took it in the shop to surgically reattach his head. I haven't seen him since. He may be in the front yard too? Do you think China and Abudabe could be there too? I'll ask around. Lay low this weekend and I'll get back with you later. Love,
Your Bro Boogie Brown.

Bro Winchester,
 Have I got a lot to share. My new word, this weekend was **REWARD**. I like it much better than consequences. Mom and Dad said I had been fairly good this week, no MAJOR problems, so we loaded up in the truck and went to the river! Can you believe it's still there! I went swimming yesterday and played so hard, I slept for about 10 hours straight. Mom was excited. Then, today I got to swim and we went out on the boat. I loved it. I wore my life jacket and they let me move around with no leash. It was fun. I missed you being there - maybe next time. I was so tired; I slept all the way home. I really like the word - reward, think I may work for another. There is no telling what they will come up with. Below is a picture because I know it is hard to believe I got a reward. All my love,
Boogie Brown.

Dear Boogie,
I think my Mom is starving me. Remember that little "intestinal" problem I told you about? Well, she was none too happy to have to clean it up at 2:30 in the morning. (I think this is early- I just napped the next day). Anyway, Mom was concerned that something was wrong, so before we went to see my girlfriend, the vet, she started starving that poor three legged disabled kitty. She moved his food off the window sill so I..... I mean he, couldn't get to it and he has to go all the way down stairs, into a room that's blocked off so he can barely fit into-to eat. Then she limited my food! She also watches when I go out to play to be sure I don't eat the flower bush that made me sick before and so I don't eat any of the groundhog droppings. But she did feed me rice and chicken. That was a good reward. I just wanted more, but Mom said no. I'm wasting away to skin and bones. Hopefully, she will feed me soon. I have enclosed a picture. I'll soon look like my monkey friend who is trying to eat too. Talk soon, Love, Winchester

Bro Winchester,
So sorry to hear you have been sick. Hasn't your Mom heard the saying starve a cold, feed a fever or is it starve a fever, and feed a cold. Either way, you didn't have either so she needs to feed you so you can get your strength back. If she doesn't feed you soon, I will get you the info on the number to call to get help. Sometimes, when Mom thinks I am sleeping, I am watching TV and these dogs come on

asking for food. If they can, you can too. Food is very important to growing boys like us. IF that dumb cat had eaten his food to start with, you wouldn't have gotten sick. Well, I am glad I got my reward this weekend because if it were today, I wouldn't have gotten one. How was I suppose to know those cords were important? Man was she upset. It seems neither the phone nor the air purifier will work without them. I just tried to cut them shorter so they wouldn't be in our way. She began yelling something about that thing killing me and I was lucky I didn't get burned. I'm not sure what she was talking about, but she got her message across loud and clear. I won't eat those cords again! Each day I seem to learn something new. It's time for bed. Talk to you soon,
Your Brother Boogie Brown.

Well Bro Winchester,
It has been a sad day here today for me. Dad and I fixed the vacuum last night. Mom was so excited. She made me go out this morning so she could move furniture and clean good. I watched from outside and that is when I saw it. Evidently, I had a Kenny the cat too all this time!!! When she cleaned behind the couch, (mind you I am not allowed back there since those stupid lamps kept falling on the floor). There he was! I couldn't tell if he had three legs or four, all I saw was his hair and can you believe it, his was the same color as mine! She sucked him right up in that vacuum cleaner. I bet he is sorry we fixed that thing. I am sorry we never got to play, maybe if we get a new play cat, I will get to play with him but, I will not eat his food. Mom says it is time for a break she has put that vacuum thing away. I can relax for a few. Until next time, Love,
Your Bro Boogie Brown.

Happy Saturday Bro Winchester,
The more I explore, the more I seem to find around here. Yesterday was no different. You are not going to believe what I found! There is this button by the door. If I touch it, Mom will stop what she is doing, look out the window, open the door, and sometimes she will let me in (sometimes she just mumbles something and closes the door). I'm

not sure what I do different to get her to let me in. I sit very nicely and wag my tail - I even smile up at her. I think the button works a lot like my collar. I'm not sure if she doesn't come to the door she gets a shock or not. She always comes and believe me I tried it out more than one time. Check by your door and see if your parents have a magic button. This is a fun way to pass the time. Talk to you soon. Love, Your Bro Boogie Brown

Dear Boogie,
Sorry I haven't written sooner. Mom has been a little off and unable to help me write. She gets these shots to help her headaches, but it causes headaches before they get better. That's kinda weird. I'm not sure if I should laugh or feel sorry for her. Just imagine you get up out of a warm bed and walk face first into a spider web. She let out with a scream, then grabbed her head and screamed some more. It kept going on. From getting the web in the face to grabbing her head, it was quite the toodoo. She is now at war with spiders and stink bugs. She is bombing the house on Saturday (I may be coming to visit). On the up side, she has been more understanding about me being sick. I now get to eat rice and beef. Mom heats it up, Dad doesn't. I'm feeling better, but I hope they don't figure it out too soon. I will let you know if we still have a house after she sets off the bomb. (You would think there would be a rule book about bombs. There are rules for everything we get into.) I hope things are going well for you. I saw that your Dad is Santa. How awesome is that? I heard he is a really important guy. Talk soon. Love your brother, Winchester

Wow Bro Winchester,
Me, Mom and Dad were getting worried since we hadn't heard from you in a while. We were going to call the weekend if we hadn't heard from you before - I'm not sure what call means, but it sounded important when Mom said it. We have those pesky spiders too. I like to play with them by stepping on them and batting them around until they stop moving. We don't like the webs either. I'm not sure about those stink bugs, that's what Mom and Dad call me when I do

something "mischievous". Come on down anytime. Your room is still empty I check it occasionally when Mom goes in there. This bomb thing sounds serious. I haven't heard of a rule on that but Mom sometimes says the living room looks like a bomb went off when all my toys are scattered around. Wonder if your Mom will throw your toys everywhere? Do bombs make loud noises? I don't like loud noises. Let me know. Dad is an important guy, he and Mom still giggle when they speak of David and the Santa experience. I'm not sure what is going on with that guy, but he seems to be pretty cool and everyone seems to like him. That pretty much describes Dad. So, maybe he is Santa. I'll check that out. I hope your Mom starts feeling better soon. Do we need to come up and take care of her? I can take her mind off her head. She may have other problems, but won't have time to be sick. Let me know if I can help. Hope to see you soon. Talk to you soon. Love,
Your Bro Boogie Brown.

Boogie Brown.
I think I'm ready, but it's supposed to rain, so Mom postponed the bombing. She said she needs to air things out afterwards. I found this hat that this fellow will loan to me. Do you think it makes me look fat? Love
Your Bro. Winchester

Love the hat Bro Winchester,
 You think you can get another so we can play Army or Navy since we love the water so much, in Abudabe or China, when we get there? We

can't talk about fat. Dad got the bright idea to weigh me this week. It meant putting me in a tub, me jumping out, putting me back, me jumping out . . . you get the idea. Finally, Mom got a reading of 83 lbs. I'm not sure what that means, but they keep calling me a Big Boy. I still like to sit in their laps, but they groan when I get there. I love to ride in Dad's truck. Sometimes he backs it out in the front yard so Mom can get in. I don't know what their problem is, I just jump right in no one has to pick me up anymore. I sit pretty still especially when they put my seat belt on. They say I can thank your Mom for that. I still haven't worked my way into their bed, but I haven't given up either. I get in it every chance I get. I got a new bed, actually it is a hand me down. It was a rug she had in front of the shower. It is soft and I haven't had time to destroy it yet. I don't think it has fluffy stuff but I will let you know when I break through the outside. I love weekends (that is what they call today), my sister comes by and Dad is usually around a lot more. My sister, Amber always brings me pig ears. I'm not sure where the rest of the pig is or even what a pig is, but his ears taste pretty good. Guess I had better go, it is hard work following all three of them all day. I'm tired. Talk to you soon. Love the hat. Love,
Bro Boogie Brown.

Dear Bro Winchester,
I am still having problems without that rulebook. How was I to know that the box under the carport was a "planter"? It wasn't doing a very good job planting. There wasn't a flower/weed or even a pot with dirt or rocks in it. Dad calmed Mom down by saying he thinks my brother Chris can fix it. I think he can fix about anything. I think I will ask him about my soccer balls that keep falling apart. Maybe I can do that tomorrow. That brings about another thing I have been pondering. Tomorrow, have you ever made it to tomorrow? I understand today and even yesterday but have never found tomorrow. Sometimes Mom and Dad say we will do something tomorrow, like go to the river. We usually get to do it but it is never on tomorrow. We went yesterday but it wasn't tomorrow. Do you think we can get to tomorrow in China or Abudabe? If you find the

rulebook or tomorrow let me know. Talk to you soon, maybe tomorrow. Love,
Your Bro Boogie Brown.

Dear Boogie,
 Mom says tomorrow is the day after today. I have another question for us to look for in the rule book. What is next week? And how do you get knocked into the middle of it. Sometimes, when Mom is sleeping and I jump in bed to say good morning, she gets upset and says she is gonna knock me into the middle of next week if I don't get off her and get out of the bedroom and let her sleep. (She is pretty grumpy when you wake her without this magic drink they call coffee). I have never tasted it but it gets Mom and Dad's eyes open in the mornings. That must be in the rule book too. I will keep looking for that rule book. Sure hope we remember all these questions when we find it. Talk to you soon. Love,
Your Bro, Winchester

Bro Winchester,
 I think our Moms are confused about time. It is the day after what she called today and now it is today. We still didn't make it to tomorrow. This being said, I think you are pretty safe not getting knocked into the middle of next week. If they can't get their days right, you know the weeks have to be a real trial. My Mom is pretty cool about me waking her up, except what she calls the middle of the night, but Dad can really lose it. I don't know what their problem with sleeping is. I can nap anytime, but when I think of something I need to do, I have to get up and run around the yard under the moon light. They don't understand. Love Boogie

PS Dad is not real happy with me today either. I have been looking for China and there are a few holes that Dad's tractor almost got stuck in and I couldn't find the rake. I didn't find China either. Dad said Abudabe is around the corner. I think I need to lay low this weekend.

Dear Boogie,

I thought I'd update you on Mom's battle with the stink bugs and spiders. Mom and Dad bombed the house yesterday. (It looked more like a fog to me) we couldn't go in the house for 3 hours. I don't know what an hour is but Dad and I cut the grass and did the yard work and then played ball and . . . well just wasted a lot of time. When we went back in... Dad went 1st and opened windows and turned fans on. There were dead bodies everywhere! (Dad says there weren't a lot, but I thought it was a feast) I was trying to help clean up and Dad put me back outside! I was playing with them before I ate them and Dad put me out before I got any to eat! Apparently, when I bite into them, they smell really bad to people. I don't think so, but hey, different opinions. I guess that's why they call them stink bugs and why Dad gets mad when Mom puts them down the garbage disposal. (I'll tell you about that thing another day) While Dad was fogging inside, Mom had a spray bottle and was spraying bugs and giggling on the deck. These things didn't go far when they just stopped moving. Their legs stopped wiggling and they were no fun to play with. Mom was trying to make a movie with her phone and she had these bugs in the way. As she went to spray them, I tried to help by getting them out of her movie. So I ate them. She got upset. I'm not sure why. Anyway, the battle was over. I gotta tell you these things aren't too smart (after the bombing one walked across Mom's clean sheets). We heard the screech outside. Mom sprayed him and is making Dad refog that room again. More to come later. Love,
Your Bro. Winchester

Hey Bro,

So glad to hear you survived the bombing. Did you get to wear that great hat? If I were you, I'd watch those parents of yours. They seem to get a thrill out of killing things even if it is only bugs - for now. When she picks that spray bottle up, you better run the other way, especially if things haven't quite been going by the stupid rule book. Sounds like the bombing thing was only a ploy to run you out of the house and get some work out of you and your Dad. Our parents just don't understand the fun we can have with those little crawling

things. I'm not sure why they get so upset when they show up. If I don't hear from you soon, I'll send help. You may want to kiss up to Mommom so if you need reinforcement, you will have someone on your side. Love,
Bro Boogie Brown

Psst! Bro Boogie, Mom got me a new toy that was supposed to be dog proof. I thought I was supposed to test it. It didn't last 3 hours. Whatever an hour is. I destuffed and desqueaked it in no time. Mom wasn't impressed. I'll send more latter. Your bro, Winchester

Wow Bro,
You are lucky! My Mom will not buy me any more toys like that. She says until I learn to appreciate them, she is not buying them. I still get bones but nothing with a squeaky thing or stuffing.
 Boogie

Good morning Bro Winchester!
 I guess I have to lay low today. Dad is looking for a bag to pack for me to go to Abudabe. That rule book sure would have helped yesterday. Mom, Dad, and Granny went to Caleb's soccer game. When they are gone, I get lonesome. I thought it would be a perfect time to clean and just knew they would be so proud. My pond was really dirty and since I am the only one using it, I thought it was my responsibility. I got to work after they left. It was such a mess. I decided to pull out the liner. Who knew it wasn't 'spose to come out? I guess the pool is now closed for the season like Uncle Jay's and

Aunt Lisa's. I'm not sure why they were so upset. I left it out in the yard for them. Picture attached. If they stay home with me or take me with them, I'll try to be good today. Will let you know how it works out. Talk to you soon. Love,
Your Bro Boogie Brown.

Wow Boogie!
 We must be connected or something. I was trying to tell Dad to fill my pool but it was upside down and I might have stepped on it a few times while trying to get his attention. Apparently this is not the kind of pool that you can jump on. It's kind of crunched in the middle. I don't think I'll ask about filling it for a while. (Like maybe until Dad fixes it-if it's fixable). Dang, that rule book sure would be handy. Maybe I should have learned to DO that sign language stuff when Mom was teaching me words instead of just learning what she was telling me with her hands. Until next time,
 Your Bro, Winchester

Hey Bro Winchester,
I've got a couple of things to share. I just got Dad to sleep and got up with Mom. I have to make a perimeter check each night just to make sure everything is OK. First, did you know if you jumped up on our door, it will come open and you can just walk right outside? Mom thought it was just a coincidence - whatever that is - but I showed her and Dad how to do it several times. That gives me lots of freedom until she remembers to lock it. The next big news is I may get a new bed. Mom was going through a sales paper and said "Bennie" - she

calls him that a lot. I just call him Dad. Anyway, she showed him a new bed for me, it cost over $100. That must be a lot of money. Dad just laughed and said he would buy it when pigs fly. Have you ever seen a pig fly? I'm not sure what a pig is but I'm going to do some research and find out where and when they fly so I can get that bed. I wonder if they use those ears that Amber buys? That is our homework. Your folks may get you one of those beds if you tell them about the pigs flying. Well I guess it is time to put Mom to bed. They are old you know and it takes a lot of sleep for them. Let me know what you find out about the pigs. Until next time,
Your Bro Boogie Brown.

Dear Boogie,
 My Dad just shook his head when Mom read your letter. He said I don't need a new bed because I sleep in bed with him when Mom's not home. Mom just gave him "the look". Does your Mom have the look? It scares me. I don't think anything scares my Dad, he just laughs. Mom asked him if he took a stupid pill. I'm not sure why anyone would do this, but it seems a lot of people do stupid things. Maybe they should stop taking those pills. I wouldn't think they are good for you. I'll keep checking on the flying pigs. They got sidetracked on the bed issue. Sometimes it's tough to keep them focused. Until next time,
Your Bro Winchester

Well Bro Winchester,
 I know I just wrote yesterday, but that was before I found out I live in a war zone. Do you live in one too? I had to send one more note and let you know. Dad told me that if I was good today we would go to the river. Well you know I had to be extra good. I never want to give up an opportunity to go swimming. So while Mom was grocery shopping, Dad and I messed around in the yard. You wouldn't believe what happened! All of a sudden these trucks started coming through our yard. Even my brother Chris came through. Some had these strange boxes on the back with dogs in them. They went in the woods with guns and dogs. The dogs would bark at me when they

came through. Some even got out and the trucks would come and pick them up. I spent all morning chasing these trucks away. I sure didn't want them to put me in the box because Dad promised the river trip. Finally we left for the river. It seemed like it took forever, but we finally made it. I helped Dad and Mr. John put the boat in the water and swam way out over my head. I met my friend Roscoe and he even played with me some. He wouldn't go in the water I think he was afraid he would mess up his new haircut his sister Julie gave him. We ran and played until way after dark. It was so much fun but I am exhausted. Guess you can tell by the picture below. I think we are safe here, but when we go back home, not sure about the war thing. Do you think your friend would let me borrow that neat hat if the war starts up back at home? I didn't hear any bombs like you had but you never know. I guess all in all it was a pretty good day once we got out of the war zone. I just worry because my sister Amber didn't come this morning. She always comes on Saturday, usually with those great pig ears. I sure hope those trucks with the dogs didn't pick her up. If she had come to our house I would have protected her. Mom and Dad didn't seem too upset so I will wait for news from her. I'll keep you posted and you keep me in your prayers for safety. This war thing is tough. Talk to you soon,
Your Bro Boogie Brown

(Boogie,
Sorry, I remembered to tell Granny I was leaving town. Next time, I'll remember to tell you. I'll make it up to you with pig ears next week...maybe candy corn too... Amber)

Amber,
Your brother was very worried about you. War is terrible when you don't know your sister is safe. Who will bring him pig ears?
Winchester

Dear Boogie,
It sounds like you had an exciting weekend. If I had known, I would have had Mom send the hat, but it sounds like you got out before you needed it. Glad to see that cousin Amber was just "being a girl" and forgot to tell you that she would be away... all that worrying for nothing. And your folks think you were so tired from playing. They don't realize you were just keeping up appearances so they would have a good time and not worry so much. They just don't know what all we do to keep them safe and worry free. Just the other day I had to supervise these guys doing yard work next door. I patrolled the fence line to be sure Mom was safe. They seemed nice enough, but I didn't let them pet me until Mom gave the OK. I still kept my eyes on them. Last night I got into a bit of trouble.... again.... I really need that rule book. Every time I chase Kenny, Mom gets really Mad. I'm beginning to think this may be a rule with no loopholes but I'll keep checking. The fly swatter coming out seemed pretty serious. Until next time,
Your Bro Winchester

(Boogie and Winchester,
There is some unfairness for me getting thrown under the bus when I have a verifiable alibi (and I told our parents where I would be)...while our other brother was witnessed being at least partially responsible for the war zone....just saying... Amber)

Bro Winchester,
I'm sending this picture to my Bro Chris and nephew Tyler. They put on siding for a living. I am wondering if they will hire me to take it off. Dad says he hopes there are no siding houses in Abudabe. It could be interesting. After he got over his surprise, threats, and tantrums, he mentioned sending me again, but decided he would

have to go, too. Then he said we would come back if we didn't like it. I'm getting mixed signals, but what came through loud and clear was: the siding - unless I get a job (hint hint) is off limits. This is another note for our rule book. Talk to you soon, I hope.
 Your Bro Boogie Brown

Bro I'm confused,
 Were you helpin' Chris and Tyler put it up? Other than a little crooked, it looks fine to me. What are they so excited about? If they're going to put you to work, they gotta expect a bit of a learning curve. Don't they? You'll have to ask about that. Love,
 Your Bro, Winchester

Silly Brother,
 You have to have thumbs to put it up. You only need teeth to take it down. Mom and Dad said the training should be on the job with Chris and Tyler (Not sure what that is, but if Chris hires me, I will find out). Keep your toes crossed - whatever that means. We have lots to explore yet.
 Bro. Boogie

Dear Boogie Brown,
 How have you been? I saw you were on the river yesterday. I thought it was a little too chilly for that, but Mom explained that you live where it stays warm, longer. We had this stuff they call frost, this week, a couple times on the grass in the morning and Moms car windows. (She said words I'm not allowed to repeat) Mom doesn't like cold, but Dad thinks it's great. I wear my coat all the time so.. I'm good. I had another near death experience this morning. Mom was not understanding-AGAIN. I was talking to Kenny through the gate at

the top of the stairs, just talking, I swear! All of a sudden the gate starts to fall over. I barely got out of the way in time. I ran to get Dad to tell him what happened and the whole time Mom was saying things like "I could've been killed; It fell all by itself; Thank goodness I got out in time; I'm so traumatized; I think I'll get Dad to protect me; He'll fix it; Maybe I'll go hide on the couch!". I think she was making fun of me! It's a good thing I have Dad trained. Mom is gonna take a bit more time. So, how is your training period with Chris and Tyler going? Are you learning a lot or just doing the demo work? Sure looks like fun. Until next time,
Your Bro Winchester

Hey Bro Winchester!
 Glad you are OK, those stairs and gates can be bad news. I think that Kenny knows it and he probably rigged it to fall. You may get your Dad to check on that. Well, I am laying low too. On Wednesday, we were getting ready for Caleb's birthday party (we still haven't had ours), I didn't have much going on, so I decided to clean the dirty thing in front of the door. It broke into a million pieces. I just picked it up and shook my head. That was not in the rule books - I'm sure! Mom was a little angry but finally settled down. Then . . . . . . On Friday, Mom left to run some errands. I decided to make up for the door mat and was just scouting the yard. All of a sudden, ... I saw this shiny thing sticking out of this box near the deck. I grab it with my teeth and ran with it. All of a sudden, this green snake thing was chasing the shiny thing. No matter where I went that snake chased me. It grew longer and longer. Finally I stopped and dropped the shiny thing and began attacking the snake. That thing was 50 feet long-no kidding! I cut it into about 10 smaller pieces. Mom and Dad do not know how I saved them that day. And would you believe . . . . Dad was so mad his tiny eyes looked like 2 red laser lights. He was almost as mad as the siding episode. He talked about packing my bag and sending me to somewhere else. I am a little worried. I wish that rule book would come in. Don't know if I will make it. Keep the door

unlocked for me I may have to make a break up north. Glad we haven't had any of that white stuff. You can keep it up there. Hope you have a Grrrreat week. Love, Your Brother Boogie Brown

Well Bro Winchester,
 Mom said I may want to let you know it has been nice being your Brother. I knew Dad was really mad when I finish off that green snake AKA water hose Monday. I found out how it was getting in that little box and cut it off from behind. I didn't pull it out this time, just the box. I am sure it died in that box. Mom and Dad just don't know how I saved them this time. That was a long snake! He says I can't be left alone. Not sure what that means, but I like being with people not sure about being with that alone dude, so I'm glad they aren't going to leave me with him. Well this morning he went to special lengths to protect me and Mom. I went out for my morning perimeter check and heard this strange noise. It was loud - sounded like that TV program MASH. I told you I lived in a war zone! It came closer and closer, you wouldn't believe It! It was up in the sky. Higher than those birds I chase. It had these things turning really fast on top and flew right over our backyard. I ran up on the deck and barked at it and ran it off. Ha! Dad thought he could keep an eye on me like that. I wonder what that big fly thing told him when they got back. I bet it was one of those things Dad works on at Cherry Point. I'm keeping an eye out in case it comes back. I am sure I can handle this thing if it does. It has to have a weakness like that snake and that is my next mission. If you see a fly thing at your house, ask them if Dad ordered its parts. Don't send it down here, I don't like them. Until next time, Love, Your Brother Boogie Brown

Dear Boogie,
I will keep my eyes peeled for those flies. They sound dangerous. You be on the lookout for escaping TV people. Love, Winchester

 PS My Mom said to tell your Dad to chill. That's what puppies do. At least, that's what my Dad tells her when she gets upset with me. Tell him to call Dad this weekend. He can splain everything!

Winchester,
 I fooled those flies today. I heard them fly over but I was in bed with
Mom on Dad's side of the bed! I protected Mom well. No problems.
 Boogie

Dear Boogie,
 Crazy things happening around here, too. Last night I was really
busy protecting Mom and Dad and then Mommom when she got
home from work. We were invaded by these creatures and people
from the TV (I gotta admit. I thought they'd be taller from watching
them on TV) some of them came a few times but they didn't fool me!
No siree! They might've been taller or shorter or heavier or younger
or older but I knew I saw them on TV! I was trying to protect
everyone and they yelled tricks and treats and Mom gave them
candy and it was like feeding strays! They kept coming back. I tried
to tell Mom that the kid Belle from the movie was here four times
and she kept giving her candy. Turtles galore. But I guess they all
look alike. I finally got them to go away about 9 o'clock. I was bushed.
The things we do to keep our families safe. I sure hope the TV doesn't
escape again tonight. Love,
Your bro, Winchester

Bro Winchester,
I didn't see any TV people at my house last night. Hope they don't
come tonight. Mom and Dad left early in the afternoon with a car
load of candy, chips, drinks, and hot dogs (Hope I'm not a hot dog
because she didn't bring any back home) for something she called
Trunk or Treat. They came home talking about all the cute little
people they saw and how nice it was for the community to pull
something like that off. I heard Mom say something about someone
cooking 1500 hot dogs. Do you think they are planning that for us?
I'm on high alert tonight. Will let you know if those TV guys escape
down here. I do like candy especially candy corn. I don't want them
giving that away. Keep in touch. Love,
Your Brother Boogie Brown

Winter

Dear Boogie,
We had a great weekend. We went to this place called Potter County to see my brand-new I guess he would be a nephew. They tell me that this critter is going to grow into a person, but right now he's smaller than Kenny. I think I could take him. He sounds like a squeaky toy but they wouldn't let me play with him. I could sniff him but they wouldn't let me play with him, and Kenny yells louder. They tell me it's going to grow into a boy, but I don't know, Shorty and Dude and Mr. C. are much bigger than this thing, and all it does is sleep and occasionally it squeaks, but they tell me it's a human baby boy, but like I said Kenny is bigger than this kid. So anyway, I also made a new friend, his name is Optimus. He is a Rotten Wyler. I'm not sure why they call him Rotten Wyler he looks like a great big dog. He is a great friend. We had fun. He has a great big pond. It's much bigger than your pond or my pool. We got to go swimming, but he was afraid and would only go up to the top of his legs. He wouldn't go swimming like you and I do in the river. He likes to dance. He climbed up on my back and would dance and dance. I had to go get a bath this morning because the grownups said his dance was in-ap-pro-pri-ate. I'm not sure what that means, but I had to go get a bath. Actually, the bath wasn't too bad. The lady was very nice. All in all, it was a good weekend. I don't think Kenny missed me. Hope your weekend was good. Love, Your Bro Winchester
PS Mom is adding a picture of me and Dad and the squeaky toy, I mean my new nephew. (Their Gran)

Wow Bro Winchester,

I've never seen a little thing like that. It looks like you are taking good care of him and your Dad. Did he bring that little thing home? I'm sure he wouldn't take up much room and could sleep in those beds we have been chewing on. As for that Rotten Wylder, did he smell bad? Anything that Mom says is rotten usually smells really bad. That is probably why you had to have a bath. Maybe we can visit him one day and teach him how to swim like we do. We have had a fairly quiet weekend. Mom cut her leg on Friday and had to go somewhere to have it sewed up. I don't know why she just didn't sew it like she used to do my toys. She said it took 9 stitches. Dad won't let me help change that thing they keep hiding it under - they call it a bandage. I could help if they would let me. Every time I get near Mom, Dad yells. He acts like she has something terrible that I may catch. She has spent most of the weekend on the couch. I haven't even been able to sit in her lap. Maybe when Dad goes to work I can slip up close to her. I did meet this pretty girl that Dad says is going to babysit me, whatever that is. I kissed her on the lips. She smelled good, nothing like that Rotten Wylder, I'm sure. I'll keep you up to date on this one. Until next time,

Your Bro Boogie Brown

Well Bro Winchester,

Have I got lots of things to tell You! First, I was soo disappointed when Mom and Dad were packing their clothes and the car and did not get my bag. I kept following them around to remind them to pack for me. I know where my bag is and they never got close to it. They left me home all alone or so I thought but later in the day, the prettiest, sweetest girl came and moved in. Her name is Emily, check out her "Spacebook".—Va-va-la-boom - young, tall, long blonde hair, the face of an angel, and a smile that makes my heart pound. She kept me fed and watered and let me in and out when I wanted. She sat on the sofa with me and let me sleep in her lap. She even used the gun to shoot off the tennis balls. What more could a puppy ask for? She slept (or tried to) at my house in the same room with me! It was hard

to sleep with her there, I was afraid I would embarrass myself (if you know what I mean). I did find out she is also one of those people running the war here. She left early to hunt something called a bear. These guys still drive me crazy going through the yard. I spend a lot of time chasing them out of the yard. I haven't seen one of those bears but if I do I will be sure to let Emily know. Maybe that will slow some traffic down. But for now, I will watch for her red truck and dream of our weekend together. By the way, Mom and Dad made it home, had a good time, blah blah. I missed them some but Emily was worth it. Talk to you soon,
Your Bro Boogie Brown.

PS: I'm not sure how long it will take them to find out about my partying while they were gone. I kept Emily up off and on all night. She wanted to sleep and I wanted to play. I sort of accidentally ate her hunting boots. They were old, now they leak too.

Winchester,
Man are you out there? I haven't heard from you in a while. They haven't sent you to Abudabe or China have they? I'm worried Bro. With our reputation, we have to keep check on each other regularly. Well if this reaches you, we had another birthday celebration yesterday - my Dad. He seemed so happy and said he got some great gifts! I know our Moms say we are going to have one but we sure have been waiting a long time. I hope they don't forget. I can get into some gifts - whatever that is. They seemed to make Dad happy. That big fly keeps coming around, but I am usually in the house. If I'm out, I come to the door and Mom lets me in. I do the same if the war breaks out behind our house, sometimes I have to ring the doorbell so she doesn't forget me. I have to protect her so I get as close as possible. I know she has to be scared. I'm not, of course. Today, Mom let me stay in most of the morning. It was cold- 32 degrees, Mom said you would laugh at that because it gets much colder up there. I don't like cold weather. I watched her collect our Kenny. Not exactly sure where she got him from but he doesn't run, just lays there and that red machine sucks him right up! I wish he would get

up and play. I still haven't seen any legs. Maybe my Kenny doesn't have ANY legs? I'll keep watching out. Guess I will close for now. I hope I hear from you soon. Love,
Boogie

Hello Boogie,
Sorry for making you worry. Mom has been working a lot and keeps forgetting to help me write. I did send your Dad a picture for his birthday of me and Dad from the summer. I haven't had any trips since we went to see my new friend Optimus and got my bath. After reading about your weekend when your folks were away.....I wanted to sing Boogie got a girlfriend but Mom said that would not be nice- Funny but not nice, so I didn't. Now about the weather... REALLY??? You have a coat on dude! Dad says 32 is just a little chilly. Mom says it's too darn cold. Anytime she has to scrape windshields, she is NOT a happy camper. I'm happy to hear that you're taking such good care of your Mom. I'm sure that fly scares her pretty bad but being the Mom she has to put on a brave front. I know Mom said our birthday is soon but I'm not sure when it is. I hope you get your presents in the mail. Keep a lookout! Until next time,
Your Bro Winchester

Dear Boogie,
Have I got a funny story for you! My sister Autumn came to stay for a few days and she brought this squeaky toy with her. It's called a chew wawa. It's smaller than Kenny and its legs are shorter than the leg Kenny doesn't have. They're even shorter than our ears! Mom can't remember his name so she calls him Pedro or the little Mexican kid but Autumn says he's an old man and I can't chew on him. I got in trouble when I tried to squeak his head. He doesn't like to play. He runs under my legs and I get all twisted up trying to follow him. I almost tied myself in a knot! Now to the funny part... Dad is not fond of . . . . (Mom is making me be nice here) little dogs. Last night, this chew baca climbed up on the sofa and curled up next to my Dad! Can you believe that? Well! You should've seen the look on Dad's face. He was not amused, but Mom sure was. She was doing that honking

thing she does when she laughs too hard and can't get air in or something. So as her eyes were leaking and she was honking and Dad was glaring... Autumn just snickered and picked up the Wookie and put him back on her lap. So the Wookie lives to squeak another day, but he still doesn't want to play, but I do get to sit with them. I am adding a picture of us. I'm the one that's cute and sexy. My Dad tells me that all the time. Hope you're doing well. Did you send your Christmas list to Santa Paws yet? I'm told he brings presents too. We'll have to check on this present thing more. Until next time, Love, Your bro Winchester

Wow Bro Winchester,
You get the neatest toys- first a Kenny now a wiggly chew toy. I don't care what your Mom or Autumn says, if his name has chew in it, his Mom knew what he was suppose to be. He sort of looks like that thing Mom called a mouse that Dad got out from under our counter. They wouldn't let me play with him either, but he didn't look like he felt too much like playing. It has been pretty nice around here. Dad has been home a bunch of days. We have played outside, gone for rides - I even went swimming in that big pond they call a river. It was a blast. They kept saying it was too cold but I had my coat on so I was good. Amber rode in the back seat with me and let me cuddle up with her. Mom brought home this little round thing that runs around the house. She calls it a "zoomba" or something like that. She seems to like it but I don't. I keep my eye on it and bark to make sure it stays

away from my family. It is really tough trying to take care of them. I'm not sure how they made it before me. As for Santa Paws, I am working on a list. Kid's keep talking to Dad about giving him a list, I'm not sure why but they seem real excited. I'll get Mom or my sister to help. Mom keeps telling me something about gifts and surprises. Boxes keep coming to our front porch. The delivery people refuse to deliver under our carport. I think it is because all the boxes are for me and they want to surprise me. I even saw one that had Chewy on it. I'm sure that was the kind of box some toys came in. Mom was quick to tell Dad she hadn't ordered anything from there yet. They must just like us. Keep your eyes open you may get a box from them too! We have a lot to do this month, protect our parents from themselves and those toys, find out about gifts, keep those pesky flies away, and since you can't chew, on chew bacca's head, you may want to try those little legs. Anywhere you chew is not going to have much meat or bones from the looks of things. Keep in touch and let me know what you learn this week. I will do the same! Until next time, Your loving Bro Boogie Brown.

Boogie! Quick update!
I may be coming to hideout!!! Chewies head fits in my mouth. It's boney and as usual... I'm in trouble. What can I say? I had to try. He didn't squeak but he sure yipped. Winchester

Dear Boogie,
My Mom got a zoom back thingy too! You gotta keep an eye on that thing. I caught it trying to eat one of my toys! My toy won. I had the rope so shredded, it tangled in the movin parts and you should've heard the words coming outta Moms mouth! It took her longer to yell than it did to fix it. She's pretty handy like that. Did you notice that when you get all comfy with your favorite bone that ole zoomy comes by and wants to bump into you? I think it wants to play, but I'm not sure. It chases Pedro. That's kinda funny. Autumn doesn't think so. She just picks ole chewie up. So. . . just wanted to give you a heads up to keep an eye on your toys. Until next time,
Your bro. Winchester

(Boogie Update- YOU should have seen the look on Winchester's face when the Roomba started pushing one of his bones around the room. He took it very personally! Winchester's Mom)

Well Bro Winchester,
I don't think I have to worry about our zoomba thing getting any rope toys. I have pretty much demolished all those a long time ago. It just loves to go under things and come out on the other side. I bark, but it doesn't affect it at all. I think I can take care of this thing, but I will have to catch Mom not looking. Well, I am literally in the dog house now. Mom and Dad left this morning and came home long after dark. I was bored and this guy came by and left a package, I swear I thought it was my birthday present. Usually they leave these packages on the front porch but since he was nice enough to leave this one within reach, I was sure it was mine. I thought he was that Santa Paws guy. I was excited and began tearing into that package. I wasn't sure why this guy would bring me a motor with an electrical cord and that bubble wrap, but I had a grand ole time. I am sure that it is in a lot more pieces now so it must be more valuable. Mom and Dad were not impressed. Dad made me get in my crate - he said for my safety. Mom said something about me earning a new pen. I'm not sure what that is but I don't think I'm going to like it and I'm even more sure that she doesn't care what I like at this time. Guess I had better close and get some rest. It looks like I am going to have to use all my charm tomorrow to get back in good graces. Talk to you soon.
Love,
Your Bro Boogie Brown.

Boogie,
Wow! This must be our day. I was chewing on a bone, minding my own business and the carpet jumped in my mouth. I didn't mean to chew on it. Mom got a bit angry, if you know what I mean. Then when I got caught chewing on it later . . .well Autumn said Mom lost her shit. (Autumn said it- I didn't) Now I didn't see any poop but I was pretty busy trying to stay a step ahead of Mom since she was

yelling was swatting at the same time. She was really mad. I guess she likes her rugs in one piece. I am keeping a low profile as well. The chair is pretty crowded with me and Autumn and Pedro. I'm hiding as best as I can. Talk to you soon. Your bro Winchester

Bro Winchester,
It happened again! Mom said "don't try to call us on the house phone" - whatever that is. It is controlled by that little box that WAS on the back of the house. That box controlled our TV too. Who knew? It was outside in my way. It looked ugly just sticking on the side of the house. How was I to know it had all that power? You guessed it, Mom left for a while today and I decided to do a little cleaning. I moved the thing Dad cooks on outside sometimes and there was that box. There were a lot of stringy things inside. Those things felt funny in my mouth. I didn't get them all the way out, but I was able to get a few untangled. I really thought I was helping. Dad doesn't have red hair, but his eyes seem to shoot fire. He was so mad he even popped me with that stupid box. I ran to Mom and stayed at her feet until he calmed down some. When he settled in and things quieted down, I got in my bed again near Mom for safety and went to sleep. Cleaning up is hard work. I heard them talking, something about a pen. I think that may be a Christmas present for me to write with. What do you think? I am still looking for that Santa Paws guy. The people that come now just go to the porch I can't get to. I'm not sure why. I will continue to lay low for a while, but would really like to get my paws on that rule book. I think it would make my life a little easier.
Until next time, Your Loving Brother Boogie Brown.

51

Bro!!!
Didn't I teach you anything??? You can't do 2-projects in 3 days, especially when they didn't appreciate the first one. Even without the book... pace yourself! I'll write more latter. Love Winchester

Dear Boogie,
 Big things happening up here. You know when it rains at your house and the water comes out of the sky? Well, up here today that water coming out of the sky was white, and fluffy, and really-really cold! I'm not sure what happened to the rain, but this stuff didn't soak into the ground it stayed on top and got really slippery. Dad called it snow. Mom is adding pictures, So when Dad and I were out in the yard today, I had a great time running around the yard and making doggy snow angels and just doing laps. Later tonight Mom tried to take me outside, but by then the snow stuff got pretty deep. I didn't want to go down the steps. I was a little scared, so I wanted to stay up on the porch and protect Mom, I mean Mom was scared. She didn't want to go down those snowy steps, so she took me out front and walked me on the sidewalk for a while. But what guy our age can pee with his Mom watching? I mean, I have my dignity! That Pedro guy staying here had problems with the snow, too. When he walked in the snow stuff, his stomach pushed the snow, on a count of his legs being so short. After a while, Mom got upset (since I didn't pee) and put me in the back yard. My feet were so cold. I didn't move an inch. When I heard my Mom at the back door, I ran right up those steps to her and in the house. I am still trying to get warm. Until later,
Your bro, Winchester

Wow Bro Winchester!

That stuff looks like the stuff Mom spilled in the kitchen when she was cooking and I ran through, only it wasn't cold. It was dry and sort of dusty. I would love to play in your yard today. I can see why chewy wouldn't like it, but tell him Mom turned on the "Zoomba" thing and it got it right up. Maybe you and Chewy could work on getting it outside. Kenny may help too. All we had was rain stuff and lots of mud. Mom and Dad make me wipe my feet when I come in and sometime even wash them, but playing in the mud is worth it. That is fine. As for being cold, didn't you have your coat on? I don't go anywhere without mine. Update on that pen thingy. It wasn't something to write with, it was something to keep me in! I really don't like it, but Mom says it is for my own good. She says I'm not safe around Dad when they come home to the surprises. I'm only trying to help! They just don't understand. Maybe one day. They only put me outside when they have to be gone a long time. Hopefully that won't happen much. Let me know how that zoomba thingy works outside. Until next time, Love,

Your Brother Boogie Brown.

Well Bro Winchester,

I am learning a lot this week. You know the pen I told you they were talking about, it wasn't to write with. It is a jail for me!! When they leave me home alone, they put me in this thing. I hate it. Dad said I worked hard for it. I'm not sure what he is talking about. I think the man that brings packages likes it. I am still in the house most of the time which is where I think I belong. I get to run and play when they are here. How is the "zoomba" thing working on that cold white stuff? Can Chewy get outside and pee now? I know that was tough. This talk of Christmas was exciting until Mom and Dad wanted me to pose for this silly picture. What do you think? I tried to cooperate in case Santa Paws was around but it has been hard. Mom says that the only birthday we have before ours is Tyler's. I know it is getting close and can't wait to par-teee! I heard your Dad say something about inviting 15 dogs to your party. I don't know that many dogs, I just hope my brother and his family and sister will come and celebrate with me. I hope Mom has the plans in the works. Guess I will close for now. Until next time, Your Brother Boogie Brown.

P.S. Hey Winchester, the mail lady brought me a Christmas card from Mr. Buddy and Mrs. Cindy. Thanks guys-it was my first one. I can't wait to meet you.

Oh Bro!
I don't know how to tell you this, but ... I think your Mom was pranking you. Mom showed me the picture and I ran before she got any ideas. She wouldn't let me take the zoomba out to play but it got a little warmer and most of the snow is going away on its own. Pedro is now able to pee without Autumn stomping a space for him to walk. I haven't seen Santa Paws but there are lots of bags n boxes in Moms sewing room. (I don't think Mom could get her sewing machine out, if there was a major tear, needing repairs, in the next month!) That room is packed tight! As for the birthday party, Mommom threatened Dad with his life if he brought 15 dogs here while she was home. She said we can party when she's at work, so I'm pretty excited. I don't know 15 dogs. I just know Pedro, Mrs. O Donnell's poodle across the street, Cliff Lee, Jack, and Backus. But I don't know what a party is, so we'll see. Maybe we can have my party this weekend when my sisters and nieces and nephews are here to celebrate Christmas with the New Jersey family and Mommom. That would be fun. I'll keep you posted. Maybe I can find directions on breaking out of jail. Until next time, Love, Winchester

Winchester,

It's almost here--our birthday!!! Mom says only a few more days!! Sure wish we had some of that white stuff down here. It's got to taste better than that (Mom says flour, whatever) stuff she dropped on the floor. Mom, Granny, Macie, & Caleb spent Friday night making goodies. They made me stay outside but not in the "Pen". I did get to taste some when they were finished and the cookies were GREAT! They kept saying I couldn't have some of it because it was chocolate (whatever that is), but it sure smelled good. Saturday Dad, Me, and Mom worked outside and in the building. The "hunters" were playing war behind our house again and I had to run them off. It was exhausting, they would leave then come right back. Guess they are "special" like my brother calls me when I do something he has told me not to do. Wonder if they have a rule book? As for the packages, I have seen Mom bring some home but they have disappeared and I promise I only ate that one! I haven't seen any pretty paper yet BUT . . . A tree appeared in our living room. It has lights and funny things hanging on it. Each time I get near it I hear No! Guess that's in the book somewhere. She has some bright pretty things setting around and doesn't let me touch them (wonder if it has to do with the thumb thingy?) I do like the ones that play music and light up. It seems to be a happy time. I'm not sure what is so funny about "the Pen". Dad talks about me doing time in "the Pen". He says I asked for it, but I don't remember asking. He put a roof and side on it, I'm not impressed. He acted like he thought I would be excited. You may wonder why I am writing this early on a Sunday. I have been up and down the past 2 nights scratching. Mom and Dad are not sure why, they say I don't have fleas. They say if Sunday night it happens again they are going to call that sweet Dr. Natalie and make an appointment. I'm ok with that, I love to ride and go to see her. She just had a birthday, maybe I can sing to her, I will definitely slip her a kiss but don't tell her husband, he may get jealous. Guess I will close for now and try to get a little more sleep. Hope your weekend has been good. Talk to you soon.

Your Brother Boogie Brown!

Happy birthday Boogie!
I'm sending some pictures of my birthday party. It was a small party. Just Mom, Mommom, Chewy, Kenny-he's the one you can't see and Me. Mommom and I didn't like the hats, Chewy didn't care. Mom got 3 different kinds of hats and made me try them all on, so she could get pictures. Parents!!! Anyway I got 3 bones. Thanks so much for the bones you sent me, they are still hanging in there. - 1 Mom got didn't survive a half hour- Mom has already written an email. I got an elephant and would you believe it???? THE RULE BOOK! Mom is gonna write about it later. Spoiler alert- there's always a catch!

Bro Winchester!!!
We made it!!! We are a whole year old, whatever that is. I saw your party post but we are partying tomorrow night. It seems I share a birthday month with Aunt Lisa, Tyler, Chase, Emily, Charlie, and Remmie. Since there are soo many of us, we are having one big party tomorrow night. I'm excited, but, Mom and Dad let me open gifts tonight. How did you know exactly what I needed? I was totally out of dinosaurs. I love them! I am sorry I missed you when you brought them. I check your room still but you are not there. I just know one day I'll go in there and you'll be there. I hope you liked your gifts too. Birthdays are worth waiting for. I hope we have another soon. I'll let you know about the party. Until next time - Happy birthday to us!!!!
Love Boogie

Bro Winchester,

It's been a long night. I got up at 2:30 to do my nightly perimeter check. All was well until I got back in the bedroom. I made my usual pass over Dad in the bed and something caught my eye. You wouldn't believe - they have another dog! There he was staring directly at me! I got between Mom and him and barked and growled at him. He mocked me by moving every time I moved. He didn't make a sound while I was looking at him. When I lay down, I heard him growl, it sounded a lot like Dad sometimes when he is asleep. Then I would jump up and bark at him again. I was trying to save Mom. Finally I sat on Mom's head and she said enough. We got up at 3:30. I have been napping since then while Mom watches Hallmark Channel. I have been watching for that handsome guy to come out. I'm sure he will have to come out sometimes. I'm not sure how long he's been here but now that I'm on to him, I'll be on high alert. I'll keep you informed.   Love you,
 Bro Boogie Brown.

Boogie Wow!
  Do you think they are going to replace you? This may be serious! So he was doing everything you did? Hmm wonder how he knew just what to do. I'll check the rule book n see if it covers replacement dogs in bed. Let me know if he's there when your Dad gets up. Love Winchester

(Hi Boogie,
You don't know us but we were wondering if we can borrow your rule book when you finish learning it? Apparently this stocking was not a chew toy. Mom should have hung it up instead of leaving it propped up by the tree. Let's just say she was not in the Christmas spirit when she saw it . . . . . your friends in the same boat. .Luke & Toby)

Hi Luke and Toby
Don't worry, just lay at your Mom's feet and look up at her very sad. Play it up! You can win her over, but I'm not sure about Santa Paws. I haven't met the guy, but I hear he checks his list. Maybe he was

checking it somewhere else when this happened. I would try to get it in the trash quick so he can't find it. As for the rule book, it seems to change, but if I ever learn, I will definitely share. Good luck on bringing her back in. I'm sure you can handle her. Do your best. Christmas will soon be here. Here's wishing you and your family a Very Merry Christmas. Mom says you have a place at the river too. Stop by ours when you are down. I'll be the one playing in the water. I love it there. Talk to you soon. Boogie

(Thanks Boogie.
Maybe we will be out of our crates by the summer and can stop by to see you at the river. I hope you & your family have a safe & Merry Christmas too. Luke & Toby)

Bro Winchester!!!
Are you up? He came! Santa Paws came! I didn't hear him at all. I was ready for him, but must have dozed off. This proves Dad doesn't know everything. He said he wasn't coming, but Mom kept telling me to believe. I believe! He must have been napping when all those strange things kept happening. If they hadn't happened, there is no telling what I may have gotten. It is OK, a little fun was worth it. Mom says I have a year now to be good. It should be easier this year, the wires are already out of the house, all the door mats are gone, the mail lady and UPS are onto me and use the front porch, there are no more flower pots, or rock pots, all the trailers with wiring have been moved, the cats don't come to play anymore, and we have "the Pen". Mom calls this Boogie proofing. Well got to go and play with all these balls! Hope you and your family have a Very Merry Christmas! Love, Your Brother Boogie Brown.

PS I can put three of those tennis balls in my mouth at once and still breathe.

Boogie,
WOW! Bro I thought I was the good brother. Maybe I need to be nicer to Kenny and Pedro. Are you sure that's all for you? I saw a lot of toys

and got to open (well tear up the paper) on some pretty sweet toys, but then Mom put them away. She said I was getting crazy. I got my treats and then the ones Pedro wouldn't eat and toys Pedro wouldn't play with. I was being nice and helping the kid out! Just showing him what to do! And the next thing you know... Mom is taking some of the toys away for later and just this situation turns up in the rule book. It's almost like the book writes itself as things go on. Who knew...? You are lucky to be an only child (yes Amber n Chris - I didn't forget about you) at home. You don't have to share...I don't like sharing on Christmas. My cousin Kristi says at one time when's she was an only... it was ALLLLL for her.   I think I would like that too.
Merry Christmas,
 Love Winchester

Psst Bro Winchester!
 I learned something new today. You know that thing our Moms push around that makes so much noise? The one your Mom snatched its head off and dumped out its brain? Well I found the key. Mom was using ours and it almost got my favorite ball and was heading straight for my bear, my bark wasn't stopping it. I had to save my bear so I grabbed that thing hanging out of the wall and pulled it. It worked! I killed it!!! It stopped making all that noise and my toys were safe. Now if only that "zoomba" thing had one of those things, I could kill it too. I'm working on a plan now if you can help me, let me know. Love,
Your Brother Boogie Brown!

(Boogie Brown.....this is your doctor speaking. Please stop pulling those things out of the wall! I don't need to see you for a SHOCKING experience! (But I'm glad your toys are safe!)
Dr. Natalie)

Bro,
 I'm telling you, the book is writing itself. No pulling plugs. You'll get shocked. Remember when you got all tingly feeling? I forget what you were fixing. But you can't kill the "zoomba" or the sucker by

yanking the plugs. We'll have to find another way. We can't risk not making our 2nd birthday party, or Santa Paws again. You need to listen to you Dr girlfriend- (Boogie got a girlfriend, Boogie got a girlfriend, hehehe) I'll ask and get back to you. Love,
Your bro. Winchester

Bro Winchester!
Lots of news for you! Our house is full! We are loving IT! I'll splain later. But that is only the beginning. That white stuff you told me about, it fell here last night! I love it!!! Since I'm not the only child now, I have someone to play with! My nephew Blazer and niece Sophie both like that snow stuff too. Blazer will run with me and play just like you did. Sophie will for a while, but she is old (Hehe like our parents) and will come in after a short time. Have you ever heard of snowed in? I'm not sure what it is because we can go out anytime we want, but I like it because Dad gets to stay home with me. A side note, since our house filled up there are a lot of good smells coming out of that room Dad says "just came with the house". They spend a lot of time with our other guests sitting around that table thing, talking and laughing (sometimes they seem a little sad too). I don't know how long this is going to last, but I love every minute (Mom and Dad do, too). I see them smiling and see the love in my Moms eyes even though she is the one in that room the most). Well gotta go, time for me and Blazer to make another run in the snow! Mom is sending pictures so you will see one of my new nephew. He has a funny nose but he is still pretty cool.
Boogie

PS. I just had my first snow cream, tasted like snow to me think Mom was fooling me, she wouldn't let me have her bowl and gave us some out of another.

Hey Boogie,
I told you it was fun! You can eat it or roll in it or just kick it up and just play. It's really cold up here and snowing too. Mom does not like this weather at all but Dad thinks it's great. Mom wants to know why

you're snowed in? You only seem to have a dusting . . . but I don't see any dust. The "Rents" sure talk funny. I'm glad you have some friends to play with but sorry they seem sad. You just need to give them all extra loving. I'll write more over the weekend. I have to go wake Dad up to go to work. Mom said to give everyone her hugs and love.
 Love n hugs too, Your bro,
Winchester

PS Boogie said his snow cream recipe wasn't right so I thought I'd pass this along to him. Winchester's Mom

Dear Boogie,
 How are things with you. Do you still have the white rain? I have a question for us to figure out. They say we may break records this weekend. Now, I haven't seen any records and let's face it, no one is better at breaking things then us, but no one is yelling at anyone to stop. Mom is saying those words about the weather, but I don't know what that has to do with records. So my first question is, what is a record? If something needs to be broken, I want in on it. My second question, do you have wind strong enough to blow small people like your Granny away? The wind up here is crazy. Mom's noisemakers on the porch have not stopped making a racket all week and they are not in tune with the neighborhood. I think I saw a bird flying backwards yesterday. Kenny won't even go outside longer than it takes to stick his body out the door, (that takes a bit Hehehe). Ouch!

Sorry Mom - I'll be nice - (I have to be nice to be allowed "Spacebook" privileges) Where was I ... he gets spooked by the "chimes" and comes right back in. Mom says your family needs some extra love this weekend so we're gonna be sending all we can, and I'm sure our "Spacebook" friends will too. Mom said she's sending prayers too. Let me know if you find the records. If I find them first, I'll send some for you and your playmates. Hope they like to break things, too.
Love your Bro,
Winchester

Bro Winchester,
If we only had those thumbs to Google about records. Mom says she googled everything and it tells her what she wants to know. I don't know what Google is either, but I like the name. I like to say it google, google, google, giggle. LOL I can't wait to get in on the action of breaking those things. Haven't been in major trouble lately so I can afford a little trouble, I guess. My main thing now is, Blazzer and I like to as Mom says, "ruff house". Not sure what that is but she yells at us to stop and gets the fly swatter if we start talking to each other loudly. I haven't heard the house bark "ruff" but maybe it is because we are making a lot of noise and can't hear it. I'll try to remember to listen out for it. As for the wind, it has slowed down a lot. Mom's music machine on the porch has been quiet last night and today but it is really cold. Not cold enough to keep me out of the pond. I went swimming 2 days this week. Dad dried me off and I came in and got under my blanket. Thanks for the extra prayers. My nephew Tyler really needs them, especially tomorrow. It looks like I am getting a new niece and 2 nephews at our house. Blazzer and Sophie will be living with us for a while. Mom and Dad say we have to get along. I have been looking for an "along" but can't find that either. You got any ideas? Maybe the alongs, the records and the rule book are all together. Anyway, I sort of like them and I think we can live in the same house. I have a lot to teach them about breaking things though. I will do my best to teach them and make sure they like it here. I know they will miss their Mom but I am willing to share mine when needed. Mom is sending pictures so you can see them. They don't

look much like me, they have funny noses but they are pretty cool and I think I can train them. Again, thanks for the extra prayers and thoughts. Tomorrow will be tough. Love, Your Bro Boogie Brown.

Bro Winchester!
Boy has it got exciting around here! It used to be quiet, just Mom and me in the daytime. Now we have my niece and nephew, Sophie and Blazzer. They have got a lot to learn! I feel sorry for them because I know they miss their house and their Mom. Their Dad comes by to visit and they really love him. He loves on them but has to go to work. Mom let's me and Blazzer go out when we get in the ruff house again. We run and play and have fun. The old lady Sophie doesn't like to play like that but she likes to explore which leads me to this morning. Mom put my and Blazzer's necklace on and let us out. Sophie came out too. After about 15 minutes I lost them, they were gone! Mom called and called them. She got in her car and rode on the woods lanes looking and calling. All of a sudden Tyler came up and he started looking too. Mom kept riding and looking and Tyler did too. Finally, Tyler with my help found them. Boy, were they in trouble! He was mad. Mom put both of them in the tub, they didn't like it. I got in the tub between the two baths. Don't know what their problem was. Water was warm and perfect. Another thing they have to learn, they have to take baths at this house. Mom says we have to go out one at a time now. She was scared. Well they are sleeping now, Mom is calming down and I am happy in the fact that finally someone else is getting in trouble. I am the good child today. Who would have thunk it. I'll keep you informed. Love,
Your Brother Boogie Brown

Dear Boogie Brown,

You didn't teach them very well. Lol They need to know the ropes. Maybe your Mom should show them how the collars work! (insert evil laugh) I can understand how everyone was very worried. Mom got real upset when she couldn't find Pedro last night. She got even more upset when she found out I was sitting on him. I would have gotten away with it but Chewy started growling and gave it away. Kenny was a big help. He just pointed and snickered. So you just enjoy the good child status. It won't last long. I have been having a bad week. I ate Chewy's bed yesterday. Dad wasn't happy and I can usually get away with murder with him. Now we both have to sleep in the crate-with no pillows! I think Chewy is setting me up. All he does is sleep on the sofa. At least you have help looking good. Well enjoy the kids and keep me posted. Love, Your Bro, Winchester

Pssst Winchester,

I got real worried, Mom put Sophie in the car and left with her today after their little trip. I was afraid she was taking her away for good. But she brought her back. She went to see my Dr. Natalie! Without ME!!! I guess it's ok though, she got shots. I wonder if those shots will make Sophie stay home? As much as I love Dr Natalie, I don't want any shots so I am staying home where I belong. I'll let you know if the shots work. Another thought, you know we may be able to send Chewy, Kenny, and Sophie to Abudabe. That may solve our problems. Check out that rule book and see if that will work. Talk to you soon! Boogie

(Hey there Boogie Brown!
I got to meet your new housemate today and she sure is a sweet heart! At least to me she was but your Mom said she kind of bosses you around. Just remember that she is a lady and may stick up for your Mom and may not always want you right on top of her! I am so glad that you are loving your new housemates and playing so good with them! Hope to see you soon- (but not too soon! I don't need you getting hurt or anything!) Take care of your friends and try to teach them to stay in the yard with you! ....Dr Natalie)

Dr. Natalie,

Boy has she got you fooled. She can really be mean to me sometimes. I just wake her up to make sure she is OK and she bites my head off. Dad said I had to get used to it. It was a "woman thing". I'm guessing that is in the rule book too. I can't believe Mom left me home today. She knows how much I love going to see you. Well I'll just have to watch closer and make sure I get in on the next trip. Until next time

Boogie Brown

Dear Boogie,

Do you know what Pedro did? I'll tell you what he did. You are not gonna believe this! I don't believe it and I'm here. Just you wait til I tell you. I just can't believe he did it. You are gonna be just as angry at him as I am. Can you believe it? Oh, I guess I better tell you first... So, the other day, ole yappy got to yapping while Dad was trying to sleep. We share a kennel in the bedroom and Dad works nights so he sleeps in the daytime. I thought I heard something and Pedro decided to think he was 10 feet tall and started yipping to beat the band and woke Dad up. Talk about lighting a fuse on stick of dynamite.... by the 2nd or 3rd time, Dad was like a crazy man. Mom even got yelled at when she got home from work. SO... that night her and Mommom brought up the old kennel from the rec room and put it in the living room so that Pedro does not have to be in the bedroom with Dad and me during the day. Mom put a couple of blankets in the kennel to pad it and Pedro just walked right in like he owned the joint! So now HE gets the cool kennel in the living room and I have to go in the bedroom kennel. (Well to be truthful Dad doesn't put me in the kennel but that's beside the point.) Pedro gets to stay in the living room for causing a ruckus! So you know what I did? Well, I'll tell you. When Mom gets home from work, I just go on in and lay down in the kennel like I am the king of the house. WHICH I AM! Then Pedro just goes and lays down next to Mom or Mommom and then I have to go and get rid of him there. I'm telling you Boogie it is tough keeping things in line up here. Hope things are good with you and your crew. Love,

Your bro, Winchester

Dear Winchester,

Man it has been a different world. Sounds like Chewy is causing as much havoc there as Sophie is here. Blazzer and I play so hard during the day. We run, roll in the grass, have been working on that hole to China, (Blazzer is as good at digging as I am), and antagonizing Sophie. She acts like she owns our house. She growls and gives me that mean look. I run and hide because I think she is crazy. Blazzer doesn't pay much attention to her. I have to watch her and eat when she gets through. Sounds like Chewy got his way, but think of it this way brother, he has to sleep alone- you get your Dad all to yourself. I think you won that battle. Luckily that is true here. Sophie and Blazzer sleep in the room you slept in and I get Mom and Dad all to myself. I love bedtime. I don't like sharing my toys or my family but, I know this is not what they wanted either. Sometimes (not often) I feel sorry for one of them and take a toy to them. Most of the time, we just coexist. The big thing is, I haven't been in much trouble since they came. I am so busy playing and resting, I don't have time for mischief. I'm sure I can work on that though. Tomorrow is a new day and now I have others to blame. Talk to you soon,

Your Brother Boogie Brown

Dear Boogie,

I finally found something that should resemble the rule book. (Not the one I got for my birthday that keeps writing itself.) Pay close attention to #7 and show it to your Mom n Dad. It should be your get out of jail free card. It 'splains everything! Mom still stands by the rule book and says no one's rule book is completely written. The future dictates how the rules write themselves. Blah blah blah. She then quoted some guy name Doc Emmett Brown - your future hasn't been written yet. No one's has. Your future is whatever you make it. I think she's losing it. Until next time, Love,

Winchester

If your dog was your teacher, these are some of the lessons you might learn:

- When loved ones come home always run to greet them
- Never pass up the opportunity to go for a joyride
- Thrive on attention and let people touch you
- When you're happy dance around and wag your entire body
- Delight in the simple joy of a long walk
- Never pretend to be something you're not
- If what you want lies buried, dig until you find it
- When someone is having a bad day, be silent, sit close by, and nuzzle them gently

Lessons Taught By Life 9/12/17

Wow Bro Winchester,
 Moms and Dads don't have a clue. I can't believe mine sometimes. First she puts that picture of me asleep on the floor and my butt did look big! Well, they woke me and Blazzer up from our sleep and sent us outside to "take care of business". I ran across a new friend! Can you believe it 3 new friends this month!!! I called Blazzer but he was so sleepy, he just went inside. I kept barking until Dad came out. My new friend was on top of my pen!!! It looked very soft and fluffy, a lot like those squeaky toys our parents used to buy us. I just knew I had found a new toy. It wouldn't come down and play. I don't understand. Tyler said it was an owl, but Dad said something about a kitten. Dad made me go inside. Tyler said "Uncle Boogie" (He he that's what he calls me)" you need to leave that thing alone". I don't understand it was my friend. Dad got the fuzzy thing down and let him run off. I stared out the window wanting to go out and play. Dad made me go to bed, but I couldn't sleep. I had a new friend and I'm sure it is waiting for me. It's not very nice to treat friends like that. Well Dad wouldn't give in, so I convinced Mom to take me out around 3 this morning and my friend had gone home. I don't blame him, if he wouldn't come out and play with me, I would leave too. I guess we will have to wait til tomorrow and I will 'splain about parents and their clueless nature to my new friend. I love making

new friends and finding their squeakers. I'll keep you updated.
Love,
 Brother Boogie Brown

Boogie.
 You have such adventures. I'm telling you. I have been getting into
such trouble this week. Mommom and I got up at the same time the
other day and I wanted to go out as she was walking and I kinda
tripped her and she fell and hit her head and banged up her knee.
Dad was really mad. (Mommom knees really bleed a lot.) I got put in
my kennel. THEN, I got bored and chewed up the quilt in the kennel.
And . . . yep got in trouble for that too. You would think my week was
complete, but noooooo. Mom takes olé Pedro and I out before bed
and I run the yard when I get done. Pedro is old and it takes him for
EV-ER. So I was running laps in the yard and it just so happened that
Pedro was in the way of the laps. So I maaay have almost tread on
him a few times and scared him. So he decided to just come back in.
(when this happens, he wakes Mom in the middle of the night to go
out) so she is a bit angry, again that he wouldn't do his business
before bed. (You shoulda seen angry at 3:30 am.) Now you'd think
she'd be mad at Pedro for that but somehow that was my fault too. I
was just sleeping I got woke up too. I just can't catch a break this
week. Luckily, Mommom was not badly hurt but she has a cut on her
knee and she is still kinda mad at me. Be careful of black kittens with
white stripes' they smell awful and make you smell bad too. Until
later, Love,
Winchester

Bro Winchester,
Have I got a job for you! The man on TV said something that made
my Mom upset. He said something about a guy named Phil in your
area saying we were going to have 6 more weeks of winter.
Something about a shadow (whatever that is) and if he saw it, it was
going to be cold longer. We may even get more of that white rain.
Well according to this guy, he saw his shadow. It has been cold
enough around here without this Phil guy causing more. Why

couldn't he just close his eyes and not see that shadow? This leads to my job for you. You think you can find that stupid rodent and wipe him out? I'm tired of this feeling cold stuff and frozen mud mess. I'm ready to go to the river and swim. His name is Punxsutawney Phil and the guy said he lived in Pennsylvania. He looked like a little guy and I think you can take him out. The guy with him had a funny looking hat and seemed excited about his "prediction". Mom was not. As for the NC side of things, Blazzer and I are best friends, but this Sophie girl is so girlie. She snaps at the littlest things. To tell the truth, I'm a little scared of her. She thinks she owns the place! She looks at me mean and I tell Mom or Dad and sometimes they yell at her, sometimes they yell at me but I tell them every time. Life is never dull around here. Let me know if you find that Phil guy.
 Lots of love,
Your Brother Boogie Brown.

Maybe this mug shot will help you find him.

Dear Boogie,
 Mom 'n I are researching this Phil guy. Can you believe this rodent has "handlers"? I wonder if he has a makeup person too. He bit his handler last year. Can't say I blame the guy. You should see my Mom if Dad wakes her up on a cold morning for something stupid. She gets really mad too. So we are checking this guy out. Love,
Your Bro Winchester

P S If you want a laugh, check out the party they have for this guy. It's not even a shadow! He stumbles around half asleep and points to a piece of paper! Dad said to tell you that we had a similar critter in the backyard last summer. That thing dug tunnels everywhere. (It also stole my red Kong toy) Dad took care of him. My Dad can do anything! Kinda like yours.

(Winchester,
You and your Mom and Dad can stay at my house! Phil is only bout an hour away. I'll help you take him out! Artemis)

Artemis,
 That is a great idea! I think this guy has some heavy security. We may need some additional help. Thanks for the offer.
 Winchester

Dear Boogie,
My Mom is very mean. Pedro started tattling about me taking his new toy. We were just playing. I mean, really! First, I'm not supposed to be mean to him, then, I'm not supposed to play with him. I can't win. But this is ridiculous! I took Pedro's new toy (it's really cool) then he came and took it back. Then the little pipsqueak had the audacity to growl! AT ME! Can you believe that? Well, the part I can't believe is how Mom settled it. She musta got tired of us playing, we were getting a little loud, so... are you ready for this? She put the toy in the slammer! That's right. She put the toy in jail and locked it! And I can't get the door open cuz believe me, I tried. And she laughed at me. I think your Mom needs to call my Mom and tell her to let the toy out of jail. After all it's not the toys fault. She'll listen to her. See if you can work on that for me. Love, Your bro, Winchester

Well Bro Winchester,
Sorry I haven't written sooner, but this week has been tough. I think I want to erase Saturdays from the lineup. I hope you got chewys toy out of the pen. I wasn't much help because that's where I spent most of my week. Last Saturday was beautiful here. Dad and Tyler put up a big pen in our yard. Mom, Amber, and Kayley went shopping. When they came back, we were all in the back yard. Well as I have told you

before, that Sophie is sooo mean to me and Blazzer. We were playing ball and she butted in. Then for NO reason, she growled and showed me her teeth. I swear that girl is BAD! I WAS SCARED! So, I jumped to get out of her way. Mom was just too close and somehow she ended up on the ground! I think Sophie scared her too. I ran to Mom's side and stayed with her. She walks funny now. Dad was mad with all of us. I'm not sure why he was mad with me, Sophie is the one that started it. Things went pretty smooth the rest of the week but Dad kept an eye on Mom all week. He wouldn't let me in her lap or anything. Then this Saturday comes. We all go outside and Blazzer and I begin playing. Mean Sophie goes inside. She is such a suck up. Well all of a sudden the outdoor cooking thing (I think Dad calls it a grill) just topples right over. It's inside spills all over the concrete. There were rocks, metal stuff, and a gas tank with a short hose attached (another story) Blazzer and I ran! We were scared! Mom wobbles out of the house and begins yelling. We run to her to come in. She starts with the fly swatter (I hate that thing). She gets me first and puts me in "the Pen". Blazzer thinks he is getting by with it but he doesn't know mom too well. He was next. We were both in "the pen". They have finally let us both back out but Dad is busy cleaning up the grill's insides and mom is taking care of her knee. Blazzer and I are going to try to stay out of trouble the rest of the day. Sophie is on her own-meany. Well until next time, Love,
Your Bro Boogie Brown

Boogie!
 You mean to tell me the grill thingy just fell over for no good reason, and you and Blaz got the fly swatter AND jail, And the guts fell out of the thingy and your Dad didn't lose his mind? (You ate the hose, didn't you?) I woulda.... I bet that ole suck up Sophie did it and snuck back in the house so you guys got blamed. Maybe SHE needs the fly swatter n jail time. Mean ole woman. She 'n Chewy would get along great. The little pipsqueak stole one of my bones this week. It was bigger than him! He got real nasty when I politely tried to get it back. These old dogs just need to be nice! Until next time, hang in there,
Your bro, Winchester

Boogie & Winchester

Pssst Brother Winchester.,

.. Don't tell anyone but my nephew Tyler figured out what he said was wrong with that mean Sophie. He says she has a crush (whatever that is) on me. I hope that doesn't mean I'm going to get hurt. Then Dad said she was a cougar (not sure what that is either). He said something about me being one (7 in dog years) and her being eight (56 in dog years). It doesn't matter, Tyler says she is flirting with me. She started wagging her tail and hiding her face. She watches me everywhere I go. I'll update you as I learn more. Love, Your Brother Boogie Brown

(Don't act like you don't know what he's talking about... I saw you two kissing the other day. Amber)

OMG. Boogie!

 Mom splained to me what they mean! She's sweet on you! Boogie's got another girlfriend. Boogie got a girlfriend. hehehe What am I laughing about? You have 3! Dr. Natalie, Miss Emily and now mean ole Sophie. You are a Casanova dude! I'm not sure if that's good or bad. Mom had a friend that she found out had a wife **and** a girlfriend. She called him a cheating rat bastard. I don't ever wanna be on the receiving end of that tone of voice. Keep me posted on the romance, Love,

Your bro, Winchester

(Boogie you just stole another heart! I guess I'll Have to share you! Dr. Natalie)

Dr. Natalie,

 I love that you keep an eye on your fans... and that you're willing to share! But I gotta tell you. My Dad says that I'm cute and sexy. So if we meet someday.... I may steal your heart away.

 Winchester

Dear Boogie,

Mom said I had to print a retraction. I'm not sure what that is but

she's telling me what to say. The word I used last night was a naughty word that told everyone her friends parents were not married at the time of their birthday. This was not the case. The parents are very nice people. The words are bass which is a fish and turd which we know is poop. So she said fish poop! (For those that are confused- see yesterday's post) I am sorry for saying something not nice about the nice people.   Love,
Winchester

Wow Bro Winchester,
Mom didn't read that word to me but I'm glad you 'splained it to me. But didn't you just say what your mom said? Maybe she needs to do a refraction or whatever that word was. I think I understand that this guy is lower than fish poop, I just know I can't use the other word because mom wouldn't tell me what it was. Mom says we are too young to use such words and she will wash my mouth out with soap. I like baths but not sure about in my mouth. Guess I won't use those words. Until next time..
Your Bro Boogie Brown

Pssst Boogie. Look at the last name for the girls!

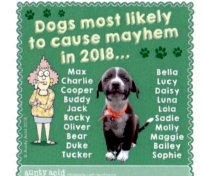

Dear Boogie,
It's been a while since I wrote so I have lots to tell you. I've been real busy keeping up with the family. I was taking care of Mommom the other week. She was at the hairdressers, Carol & Sis & Michelle are great, anyway, she bent over to pick up her glove and her coat

pushed her over. (The coat was in timeout for a few days. That is Mommom's story n she's sticking to it) 7 stitches later and I took really good care of her. Just ask her. Then we had this big tadoo up here when these birds won a bowl with a ball that's not round. The other year it wasn't filled up but that's another story. You shoulda seen the pictures on the TV box. These birds (that aren't birds, they are big guys playing with a ball) won a game and people busted up the town. On the TV they showed a bunch of pictures of people, that some guy, called the mayor, said were on the list of knuckleheads, that forgot everything is on somebody's phone these days. Well. Mom heard of the knucklehead list and spit her drink across the room cuz she was laughing and I had to clean the TV from the splash. My work is never done! I did get a laugh break, when Chewy had to get his nails clipped. Once, I got a tad too close with my heckling and Mom got mad and said "I can do you next if you don't back off". I thought she was kidding til she grabbed my foot. I decided to go protect Mommom til she finished. The clippy noise was scaring her. So that about updates us. I been hearing talk about bike week so I'm on my best behavior. I've never been to bike week but last year on the way back is when mom n dad adopted me. Do you think they'll bring another kid home this year? I hope they just take me and bring me to see you. Here's hoping. Love,
Your Bro, Winchester

PS Yesterday I had to help my Great Niece Kristi take Mommom's stitches out. If I hadn't given such great instructions, those strings would never come out! What would they do without me??? Dad held the light, & Zippy ate his lunch. We all had our jobs to do.

Well Bro Winchester,
 Mom never ceases to amaze me! She was looking at that "Spacebook" thing and made me come over and look. She was laughing about this picture. Guess where it is!! ABUDABE!!!! Just when I think she is making up a place, it shows up on that "Spacebook". Like it is reading my mind. She said me and you could slide for days on that floor, something called "marble". If it was that good, you would think some other dogs would be there. This time it wasn't reading our mind though. Mom's cousin **Heather** went there! I'm not sure what she did to get sent there. It must have been terrible!! I know every time I seem to get in trouble Mom tells me to pack my bags, she is sending me there. From Heather's pictures, it looks like a nice place just not sure why it is a threat. Maybe just a vacation break for all of us? Guess I will have to check with Heather and find out how to get a vacation there. Maybe Mom and Dad need one there. I need to do some more investigation. If you know someone that has gone there, check with them too. I'm not sure when they will release Heather to talk. Guess it depends on her offense. Hope you, Chewy and your family are all ok. Talk to you soon. Love,
Your Brother Boogie Brown

Wow!
 That is some punishment! You know what? It's probably a trick. We'd do one slide and get in trouble for scratching it up or

something. But it's real pretty. Check with Heather and see if they made her polish the floors before or after sliding, cuz you can't visit floors like that and not slide. . can you??? I don't think so. Get back to me on that. Love,
 Winchester

Hey Bro Winchester,
We have lots to catch up on. Things around here have been pretty calm for me until yesterday. (I'll get to that later) Sophie is still being mean most of the time but occasionally will get close to me and I kiss her on the ear. (Don't tell Dad but I kissed her on the mouth one time too). Dad and Tyler pick on me so I keep it on the down low. Mom thinks it's cute. Blazer is keeping a lot of heat off me by digging. He says he is digging trying to see you but we both know he can't do that. He is so naive. He may reach China though, the last hole is big enough to get my whole head in. Dad and Ty keep filling them in. I don't like the stuff they put in the hole so I have left the digging to him. This all leads us to last night. Mom cooked something she called a beef roast that smelled good all day. Blazer and I sniffed in the smell every time we went through the kitchen. She and Dad ate and put the leftovers on the stove for Tyler. Mistake number one. They let me and Blazer in and we made our trip around the kitchen. Mistake number two. It was the strangest thing. This beef roast whatever that was just took flight. The spoon flew through the air and on it was about 2 lbs (according to Mom) of meat. Well Blazer and I knew we would be blamed for something so we immediately began cleaning the floor. The only way to clean it up was to eat it. We didn't want to but we knew we had to clean it up. Unfortunately, we didn't get it cleaned in time. Dad came in and would you believe, he grabbed the spoon, popped Blazer and me on the butt with it and sent us to our beds. We were only trying to help (I told you we would get blamed). We did get all the meat up but Sophie and Dad got the juice and potatoes. Today will be a lay low day, don't want to run up with that dumb spoon again. It got us in trouble then hit us. I'm through with that thing. Until next time, Love
Your Brother Boogie Brown

Oh no!!   Not the spoon! Your Dad is pure evil. Didn't you tell him you were just cleaning up the mess? Wow some parents. You should've blamed ole Sophie.
Winchester

Psst Bro Winchester,
I was Eardropping, yes I meant eardropping- I heard it with my own 2 ears. Mom was on the phone with your mom, you won't believe what I heard, don't tell anyone---- you are coming here next week!!!! Can you believe it? Have you found next week? I know we talked about it before and you said something about getting knocked into the middle of next week. We don't want to get to the middle, just Next Weekend!!! My brother Chris is having a birthday and we were planning on celebrating it-now you can come. I am so excited, I am going to help Mom get your room ready. We are getting the front bedroom ready for you since Tyler is in your old room. Be VERY VERY good, we don't want them to change their minds. You will get to meet my new friends. It will be so much fun. I can't wait to see you. Remember to keep it on the downlow. I don't think you are 'spose to eardrop but I could not help it. The conversation sounded too interesting. See you soon.
Love your Brother Boogie Brown!!!

Boogie,
Oh...... I guess that Lebanon bologna wasn't for me. Oops. Mom knows it's my favorite! I wasn't sure what she meant when she said it was for me to take to cousin, Bennie. I guess I wasn't apposed to eat it. It was really good. I sure hope Mom can get more. I mean how was I supposed to know??? Maybe your Mom can call my Mom. This down low stuff just isn't fair! How was I supposed to know to be good??? Aw man. I'm gonna have to really do some damage control. Maybe not eat your bones or something..... cross your fingers Oh we don't have any ... crap. Well wish me luck. Love
Winchester.

Bro Winchester!

Have you packed your bags yet?? Mom says it's Tuesday!! Not sure what that means but she showed me the day you were coming on the silly clock she has. It doesn't look too far away. Remember, bring lots of toys! Mom bought some Better Than Ears for us. She says she has your room ready and is not letting us back in there. She even scrubbed the floor and said it was off-limits to us. Maybe she will let y'all in. I am sooo excited! We will have lots of room to run and play. We will probably not go to the river they say it is too cold. I don't think so because we have our coats all the time. Wish they had coats like that so we could go more. But--I'm sure we will find plenty of mischief (as my mail lady says) to get into. I have been telling Blazzer and Sophie but they don't seem as excited as I am. You will like Blazzer but we will have to work around Sophie. I'm getting pretty good at that until she gets in a better mood and lets me get near her. She's so finicky. Anyway I'm counting the days! We are down to one paw!! See you soon!!! Boogie!

Boogie,

 A disaster! That white rain is coming and people are losing their minds! Something about a nor Easter. I thought that was a rabbit but 10-14 inches. (Is that a lot?) Mom says we could lose Pedro. She says it like it's a bad thing. Can you imagine just his tail showing as he tunnels through the yard, I'll send pictures, more later. (Mom says the storm should fizzle out and just get on with spring but I wanna see Pedro tunnel).

Winchester

Winchester,

 I'm not sure about inches either but when Mom read your response, Tyler piped up and said don't bring it down here! Imagine the muddy mess we could make with Blazzer! That could be fun! Hope this disaster doesn't hold up your trip! Boogie

Boogie,

Tyler has no sense of adventure! But he can still look at the pictures.

Mom said to ask if he wants a snowball? (They aren't very good balls. You bite into 'em and they squish and they are cold and don't roll or anything) Winchester

PS Mom said she's out of here ASAP Friday. Dad is to have the car packed including me when she gets home from work.
Winchester

Winchester,
Send pictures, Tyler will love it. Pack a few snow balls, we can pick on the old lady with them. You need to help your Dad, maybe just get in the car that morning so they don't forget you.
Boogie

WINCHESTER!!!
TODAY IS FRIDAY!!! ONE MORE TOE AND YOU WILL BE HERE!!! Are you in the car yet? I still haven't found tomorrow but Mom says when that silly clock shows Saturday, you will be here. I think I will stay up all night and wait. You even get to be here when the whole crew is here. You will get to sing Happy Birthday to my brother and try Granny's famous banana pudding. We have lots to catch up on. Dad says don't forget that lebonan bologna whatever that is. I will make a scan of the yard. There are a lot of limbs for us to chew on. I'm so excited. No sleep for me and probably the folks. HURRY!!
Boogie

Boogie,
I just wrote to you. Guess we think alike. Shocker. Mom says that a lot. I have a question for you. What is a banana pudding? I'm sure if your Granny made it, it is food and it's good. (Mom n Dad, well Mom more than Dad, don't let me eat their food) the lady vet, the other night, said I was overweight! I weigh 92 and she said I need to lose 7 pounds. Dad said it is winter weight cuz we can't play in the mud. So maybe I can taste a banana pudding and run around with you and the other kids and that will lose my Chubb hub, whatever that is. Dad says I'm still cute n sexy so it's ok. I will call every hour on the way.

Oh... mom says that isn't happening. I guess I'll knock on the door when we arrive if you're not awake. See you soon. Love, Winchester

BOOGIE!
Mom's getting clothes together! (It would be so much easier if they just wore the same coat all the time like we do. SMH- that means shake my head.) She is making lists so she doesn't forget. She got a little upset when I tried to add my name to the list cuz I can't write. I don't want her to forget me!! She called me Bigfoot! Can you believe that? I didn't argue cuz it's 1 toe day. I wasn't supposed to snoop but she got bones at the butcher and they're really good. Chewy n I have been quality checking the itty bitty ones. Dad says we have to bring the truck so everything fits. Mom told Mommom everything fit the last 2 visits in the car but she wasn't arguing either. Do you think Dad would leave her at home? I am so excited and I keep trying to dance with Pedro and he doesn't dance so good and gets upset when I step on him. He needs to learn to dance, without snapping n growling. (He looks pretty silly) Dad says we should be there in the morning. Whatever that is.... See you soon. I'm so excited.
Love, Winchester

WINCHESTER,
Don't let your Dad get to you. Mom says a big foot means we have a good foundation (whatever that is). I sure hope your Dad doesn't leave your Mom, because my Mom is looking forward to seeing her. When you get here we can dance. I'm pretty good if I do say so myself. Don't count on the old lady, she's not going to dance either. Mom is making a casserole for breakfast so you can eat when you get here. I guess breakfast time is when you'll be here. Maybe if we go to sleep when we wake up, you will be here. I'm so excited, I'm not sure if I can sleep. Mom says when we see the sun again you will be here. I'm looking for the sun now. I can't wait. Love, Boogie Brown!

Bro Winchester!
I just got up to look for the sun and you. Mom tried to tell me you weren't here that it is only 1 am (whatever that means) but I had to

get up and see for myself. I couldn't find either of you. I am soo excited!! Also, there is this wonderful smell coming out of the room that came with the house. Mom says it is a sausage casserole. I'm not sure what that is but if it tastes as good as it smells, we are in for a treat. I have checked the perimeter and Mom is going to try to get me back in bed. I may try to rest a few before you get here. HURRY! Tell your Dad to put the pedal to the medal (whatever that means, I heard it on a movie on TV). Love, Bro Boogie Brown

Boogie,
We just went to leave and the truck battery is dead!!!!! Dad says not to worry. He is gonna charge it for an hour and then we're off! Don't wait on us to eat. We'll get there ASAP.
Winchester
Ok well, give it CPR or a shock or whatever it takes. We have some serious play, I mean work to do.
Boogie

Boogie,
Leaving now, see you when we get there! Winchester

WINCHESTER,
The sun is here, where are YOU!! I have looked all through the house except the room Mom got ready for you, because it is still off limits. Blazzer and I searched the yard except the front because that is off limits too. I even looked where Blazzer looked to make sure he didn't miss you. Just a little warning, the old lady Sophie is ill today. She just snapped at me because I woke her to make sure she was ok. Women@!#$!@#. HURRY! BUT BE CAREFUL!
Boogie

 Morning Boogie,
We're getting close. Mom says we're 64 miles away. (tomorrow, next week, miles, days, toe days. How are we supposed to understand all this stuff???)   All I know is that its light out and I'm still in the backseat, but I'm being good cuz I don't want Dad to turn the truck

around. On a movie on the TV box, the kids were misbehaving and the dad said he was gonna turn the car around and go back home! So I'm not making a sound. See you soon. Love,
Winchester.

PS only 58 miles now

Dear Mommom,
I'm sure you're missing me since I've been gone. I got down to Boogie's house yesterday morning. It's been great fun. I got to meet Blazzer and Sophie. Blazzer is just like one of the guys but Sophie hasn't been feeling so good she has Arthur- itez and he makes her leg hurt. (I don't know why Uncle Bennie doesn't just make Arthur leave if he's hurting her.) She seems ok when she's not snapping and growling. We played and played but had to go to jail when Dad 'n Bennie went to clean fish and Mom 'n Aunt Wendy went to get cupcakes for the birthday party today!!! Boogie and I are gonna dance and sing it will such fun! More later. Try not to miss me too much. Love, Winchester

Boogie!
Look what we found on our trip. They have a fort named after Pedro! Mom isn't fast enough with her camera and it's raining so she's sending this picture. I had a great time this weekend. Thanks for having us. See you again in a week. (I pouted so much this morning they are bringing me back to visit on the way home) who said we don't have them trained??? Love, Bro Winchester

WINCHESTER!
Did you bring your cool hat? Did they take you to join the Mexican Army? I knew something was up when Cousin Mike stuffed you in the truck and wouldn't let me in. I tried to save you! When Mom made me come in, I got on the couch and began pouting too. The next thing I knew, my eyes were closed and I was dreaming of the fun we had running, playing ball, aggravating our Dads by not bringing the balls back, and picking on Sophie. Blazzer and I just came back in from looking for you. The truck was gone, but I had no idea they were going to enlist you. DON'T, by any means, put your paw print on anything!! They will keep you Dude! I will be watching for you to come back. If you don't get here within the week, I'll put out a Chesador Alert!! Code Red!! Keep in touch so I know you are safe. Have fun and see you soon. Love, Boogie Brown

Bro Winchester,
You wouldn't believe it but . . . The night you left, some of that white rain came. Amber said she asked you to leave it up there and since you didn't it was rude to leave the State before it got here. Wish you had been here, Blazzer will play a little while but doesn't like to get wet like we do. Sophie is not interested at all. (You know how old people are). Mom said you got there safe and did not enlist. Be careful because on the way back you have to come by that Mexican Fort again. Remember no paw prints on anything. Hope you are having fun in Florida, Mom promised to let me know when you are heading back. See you soon. Love, Your Brother Boogie Brown

Dear Boogie.
I made a new friend to nap in the sun with and have a nice soft pillow too! Having fun on my vacation, I'm not sure why we don't do this all the time. See you soon. Love, Winchester

Boogie & Winchester

Winchester,
Be careful in that sun, you are already dark enough. Your new friend looks nice. He has a beard like our Dads. Has he taken you for a ride on that motorcycle yet. I think that would be fun. Hope you brought your war helmet. Be careful, hope to see you soon. Remember NO paw prints on anything, it's a trap.
Boogie

Bro Winchester,
Hurry back soon! Mom has gone wild. You know those great nose and paw prints we put on the back door? She wiped them off! Can you believe it? We worked hard to make them just right. They are all gone!! Some people just don't appreciate art. Well, when I realized she wasn't going to stop (even though I took the roll of paper towels and ran), and she finished outside and went inside, I began helping again. As she wiped the inside, I licked the outside. She wouldn't let me keep the paper towels. She wasn't pleased-not sure when she is going to learn. We did the same thing the last few times. Hope you are having fun in Florida. It is finally warming up a little here. See you soon. Love, Boogie Brown

Boogie,
What is it with Moms and art work? My Mom puts pictures that my nieces n nephews make, up on the big box with food in it, but she 'n Mommom both wipe off the nose 'n paw works of art that I spend so much time perfecting. I just don't get it. I heard Mom 'n Dad talking

and we'll be back on toes day to see you before going home. We can make more pictures for your Mom. She's a tough critic... I'm having a good time here teaching my new friends to play ball but I'll be glad to get back to some bro time. See you soon. Love, Winchester

Oooh Bro Winchester!
Mom said the 4 letter "S" word today and she even went to church. She said you were coming on "toes"day night and bringing the "S" on Wednesday!! She said she asked for Florida Sunshine and you are bringing SNOW! I am sooo excited. If it comes, we can run and play in it. Old Sophie won't play with me but Blazzer can keep up with us. Dad said something about dusting, but that is housework. Snow is on the outside, silly Dad. Hurry back so we can get this party started! See you "Toes"day! Love
 Boogie

Boogie,
Our Moms have potty mouths! My Mom didn't go to church but she read your letter and said the "S" word 3 times! (She didn't say snow) It's been really warm here yesterday and today. My Mom gets really red in the sun when it's warm. She puts this stuff on her face n arms to keep from burning but forgot her feet. Even her toes are bright red. She said shoes are not gonna be fun. (I never figured out why they wear them anyway) oh well. See you "toes"day. Love,
Winchester

Bro Winchester!
 Where are you? That funny clock says it is "Toes"day. You are not here! I have searched the yard, Blazzer has looked for you. Your truck is not here either. I even took a nap hoping you would be here when I woke up. Sophie is asleep on the couch. She's not too worried. I am. I have my balls piled up waiting for you. I'm ready to play. HURRY!! Boogie

Boogie,
We're on our way. We just passed that fun guy I showed you before but No Paw prints! Dad says we're in the same state. Whatever that means. But "toes" day isn't over yet and we'll get there soon. I'll try the nap thing and see if that works. Love,
Winchester

Boogie!
Dad said we're 38 my's out. I said "my" a bunch of times but we're still not there. Do you know how much 38 is? Or what a "my" is? We will need to talk about this when we get there. Warm up the balls. See you soon! Winchester

This pretty much sums up our first year of life. As you can tell, Winchester and I have had some adventures. We have had highs and lows. The highs were way high, soft beds, warm house, places to swim, and lots of food and toys. The lows included "the Pen", learning patience, putting up with lots of kids and having to say goodbye to some. Winchester and I have decided to never say "goodbye" but "See you later" or "Until next time" each time. We know our folks will help us get together again soon.

Stay tuned for Year Two. It has already started with a bang. Winchester has Chewy and Mommom living with him and I have Blazzer, Sophie, and Tyler living with me. Our adventures are just beginning. Hold onto your teeth Mom and Dad. You are in for the ride of your life!

Boogie Brown, Winchester, and their Moms

Made in the USA
Lexington, KY
10 June 2018